D0181314

WE WERE WITH ST. FRANCIS

An early franciscan story
edited and translated by
SALVATOR BUTLER O. F. M.

EDIZIONI PORZIUNCOLA

We Were with St. Francis by SALVATOR BUTLER O.F.M.
Translated from the Latin text published in *I fiori dei tre compagni* by *Jacques Cambell O.F.M.*, Milan, Società Editrice Vita e Pensiero, 1967.

ALL RIGHTS RESERVED

First printing, 1976
Sixth reprinting, 2003

Imprimatur:
Fr. JOHANNES BOCCALI
Minister Provincialis
ac Legati Pontificii Portiunculae Delegatus

S. Mariae Angelorum, die 25 Martii 1984

© Edizioni Porziuncola
 Via Protomartiri Francescani, 2
 06088 Santa Maria degli Angeli (Pg)

ISBN 88-270-0062-3

CONTENTS

Introduction   IX
The text, its translation, and its order   XVIII
Peculiarities of vocabulary   XX

The narrative

Letter of presentation   3
St. Francis nearing death is brought to Assisi   5
God's love justifies begging   7
St. Francis is a guest of the Lord Bishop of Ostia   8
The companions are taught to beg   11
St. Francis at the bishop's palace   13
St. Francis is informed of his imminent death   15
St. Francis declares his intentions on the rule   16
The little flock   17
St. Francis teaches the brothers a salutation   18
The Lord wanted a people who want only him   19
The companions add their testimony to Brother Richer's   20
The dangers of learning   23

Again the brother wanting a book 28

St. Francis explains his toleration of aberrations and his
    resignation 29

A last supper and a blessing 34

Parsley picked in the dark 35

St. Francis foresees that his body will be venerated as
    a relic 37

St. Francis satisfies a companion's wish for a relic 38

St. Francis writes a script for his companion 39

St. Francis blesses Assisi 40

The will to die in absolute poverty 41

St. Francis sings a new song because Sister Death is
    coming 43

The arrival of Lady Jacoba 45

He had wisely built upon humility and poverty 48

Brother Bernard is first in St. Francis's love 53

Lady Clare sees St. Francis the last time 57

The larks' adieu 59

Demons in the Lord's service 61

Both graces and torments on Mount Alverna 66

The devil slyly hides in a pillow 68

Spiritual training of the early brothers 73

Thoughtful regard for a sick brother 78

St. Francis in prayer 79

Compassionate help to a tempted brother 80

The need of a church 81

The Benedictines grant St. Mary of the Angels to the
brothers   82

Some information on St. Mary of the Angels   83

Exemplary life at St. Mary of the Angels   86

St. Francis's mind on cells and houses   88

Directions on the erection of friaries   93

The Saint speaks while expecting death at Siena   97

St. Francis loves a simple brother   99

St. Francis in temptation   103

St. Francis makes amends for a leper's hurt feelings   105

Lucifer's vacant throne is reserved for St. Francis   107

The singular meeting of Pacificus with St. Francis   109

The Saint's teaching on work and disciplined speech   11i

The brothers are sent to foreign countries   113

The demons are driven out of Arezzo   116

The Bishop of Ostia forbids St. Francis's journey to
France   117

St. Francis explains his conscience as superior   119

Sister Locust sings for St. Francis   120

The Saint chooses good example instead of warm
clothing   122

The Lord not St. Francis rules the Order   123

St. Francis's obligations to the Order after resignation 125

An example of St. Francis's earnest faithfulness to
poverty   126

The mirror of the Incarnate Christ   127

St. Francis reads a brother's secret thoughts 128

St. Francis perceives a brother's state of soul 129

St. Francis comprehends Brother Bandits 130

An innocent lamb's death is avenged 133

St. Francis perceives guile behind the pious appearances
of a brother 134

An angel plays music for St. Francis 136

A miraculous vintage rewards a priest's forbearance 138

A fine meal is served to St. Francis's doctor 140

St. Francis reconciles a cruel husband with his wife and
the Lord 142

The plea of a young nobleman is rejected 144

Proper food is brought to ailing St. Francis 145

St. Francis discerns the thoughts of a humiliated companion 146

St. Francis comes forth from seclusion to bless an unan-
nounced brother 147

A lesson on poverty and humility on the feast of our
Lord's Nativity 149

The future Pope Gregory IX is given a practical lesson
on gospel poverty 151

St. Francis is pleased with the place and the people at
Greccio 152

St. Francis preaches peace to the Perugians 155

In answer to the Saint's prayer an abbot receives a grace 157

St. Francis's keen sympathy for the suffering Jesus
Christ 159

The Saint's absolute candor in fulfilling his duty of being an example   161

The composition of the *Canticle of Brother Sun* at St. Damien's   166

St. Francis explains the use to be made of his *Canticle*   171

St. Francis composes a stanza on pardon for his *Canticle*   173

St. Francis sends a message with a song to the Poor Clares   175

St. Francis goes to Fonte Colombo for eye treatment   177

Brother Fire is gentle during the cautery   179

St. Francis's regard for fire and other creatures   180

St. Francis aids a needy woman   183

Some examples of zealous poverty and joyful charity   185

Two miraculous cures and a prophecy   190

The Lord answers a question for St. Francis   192

INDICES

TOPICAL INDEX (a guide to key themes in the narrative)   193

INDEX OF PERSONS AND PLACES   223

INTRODUCTION

This book bears a bold title: *We Were with St. Francis.*
It is a set of rambling stories, artlessly written up, but
recorded by men who had shared the daily life of the
celebrated saint. The title has then its justification.

These men were three of St. Francis's dearest companions. One was his confidant and confessor, Brother
Leo, who was also his nurse in his final illnesses. Another
was a brother given extravagantly to the life of the spirit,
Brother Rufinus, whom he called a saint, and liked to
have near him. The other was a gentle, beloved friend,
Brother Angelus, who was his Guardian in later years.
A day came when they were called upon to report on
their spiritual father. With a will they wrote down the
wonders only they had known until then about their
brother, father, and holy master. Their writing took the
form of a narrative made up of keenly significant tales,
that after more than seven hundred years can still draw
their readers into the orbit of the saintly man they knew
so well.

Let them then talk to men of today. No Catholic saint
has won interest and affection around the world as
St. Francis has. In our present society, weighted with

materialism, frustrated by doubts, and mushrooming with ephemeral ideologies, St. Francis is being looked to in hope for guidance in renewing religious aspirations. Ours is also a time when the whole question of Franciscan life is being reviewed, and although the followers of St. Francis, if they are to follow the Spirit, may not be expected to identify their individual vocations with the career to which St. Francis was called, their inquiries will be considerably simplified if when speaking of St. Francis they are enabled to speak of him with assurance as he really was.

He charms us by his conversations with brother and sister Creatures whom the Lord had made exceedingly good and beautiful; he warms our hearts and loosens our purse-strings with his anxiousness to give whatever he had on his back to any needy man he came upon; he overawes us with his ineffably sublime encounter with the Seraph on Mount Alverna. One could almost say he is too attractive; he is too lovable, and is loved rather than listened to. We can make of him a myth, a beautiful, ever so edifying myth, but nevertheless not the image of St. Francis, the man, who had paid beyond all measure in deprivations so as to make of himself and his actions a dramatic re-presentation of what the Lord of the Gospel teaches perennially to all mankind.

The companions' tales are a sobering remedy to complaisance in sacred imaginings. They depict their holy master in his true outlines and tell us his motives and aims as he himself had defined them.

Their stories are not altogether new to us. They

have supplied material for both ancient and recent narratives on St. Francis, and versions of the stories published in this volume already exist in English translation. This book has been prepared in form and manner of writing to make the companions' tales readily accessible to readers wishing to gain by their reading not so much learning in Franciscanism, as a surer, more intimate awareness of the man St. Francis was and nothing else.

St. Francis is exceptional among medieval saints for the quantity and quality of documentary material drawn up while he lived or while the influence of his person was still being felt. We of the present day have a distinct advantage. From the dawn of the century highly competent scholars have been working on source texts. Excellent and reliable studies on St. Francis have been published for the use of anyone wishing to be enlightened on this exemplar of the gospel life. Why then resort to the companions' tales that masters of Franciscanism have largely left in shadow ?

Surely the narrative merits a hearing if the authors actually lived side by side with the saintly subject of their narration, and if they were eye-witnesses and even participants in the tales recorded. But were they ? They do not hesitate to insist and insist again that they were just that, and they could hardly offer better credentials than their lack of literary acumen combined with their failure to exhibit any intellectual prowess. They were not interested in the art of writing, but they leave no doubt that they knew what they were writing about.

Their report that has much to say about St. Francis is not a biography. The narrative follows no chronological sequence, as will become evident in the very first tale where already the Saint is spoken of with reference to his approaching death. The loosely strung stories can be serviceable only to persons already acquainted with the life of St. Francis of Assisi. Substantially it is a collection of reports lifted from a Latin manuscript where it had been included among a miscellany of Franciscan writings. The manuscript is preserved in the *Biblioteca Augusta Comunale* at Perugia. It is a scribe's copy of works already existing, and was executed in or close to the year 1311.

The narrative was little known when it was brought to light by Fr. Ferdinand Delorme who made a first publication of it in 1922. Since then it has acquired the appellation of the *Legend of Perugia*. Actually the word *legend* is a misnomer applied to the work for lack of a more apt term, for it is not a *legenda* in the medieval sense. A *legenda* was a formal literary composition intended to be read and reread for the purpose of edification. Conventional norms, including an orderly exposition, were expected of such a work, and they are wanting in the *Legend of Perugia*.

During its twentieth century history it has engaged the interests of various specialists and learned authors in the field of Franciscanism. For some scholars it was a tantalizing find because there were reasons for linking it with the name of Brother Leo, whose name is conspicuous in early Franciscan vicissitudes, and who is a subject of historical enigmas in his own right. In recent years two scholars, Fr. Jacques Cambell O.F.M., and Mrs. Rosalind B. Brooke, have investigated all that can be known of ancient copies of the same narrative, or passages of it, to be found in early manuscripts, and have dedicated their specialized talents to a study of their correlation with the Perugia text. Each has published a rectified version of that series of stories. We now have available two versions, which although not necessarily complete, approximate the original Latin manuscript. They carried out their considerable labors altogether independently one of the other and finally, it would seem from their comments, to the surprise of one another. May they be rewarded with our warm appreciation for their labor of love.

They have justified a feature of prime interest regarding the present volume. It is the inclusion of the letter written by the Brothers Leo, Rufinus and Angelus to their Minister General, Brother Crescentius, in the year 1246. Customarily the letter has been used to introduce the well known *Legend of the Three Companions* where it serves the purpose awkwardly. As a description of that narrative it is puzzling. Most pointedly, the *Legend of the Three Companions* answers to the requirements of a *legenda*, whereas in that introductory letter the writers speak of reports chosen at random, as one would pluck the prettiest flowers first here and then there, as they felt free to do because they were hoping their information would be given the dignity of literary formalities at the hand of another; an expert writer would be glad to get it to enrich a biography — as Thomas of Celano was soon to do. Thus they are understood to be submitting stories to Brother Crescentius and not to a reading public. The Perugia stories with their wandering sequence and their styless style follow very naturally in the wake of that letter.

The companions had said they would report on miracles. After a straightforward report of a remarkable event, they are likely to state that they, at times together with other brothers, perhaps lay persons — even distinguished ones — were amazed at St. Francis's great holiness and that all of them concurred in declaring that this was a miracle. Thus the Minister General is advised that here is one of the miracles he with the General Chapter had solicited from brothers like themselves.

There is even room for keenly regretting that the stories respond too faithfully to the specifications set down in the letter. The companions announce that they will give information beyond what had been requested on miracles, but being careful not to repeat what excellent writers had already made known. They kept their word. If only they had been less conscientious! They could have gone on to narrate and tell us many more precious details on a living, breathing St. Francis. For instance, one of those companions would have had wonderful things to say about his holy Father's encounter with the Seraph. Instead, when the St. Michael's Lent on Mount Alverna is dealt with, this stupendous event is merely mentioned and passed over: the story had already been artfully and brilliantly written by Thomas of Celano.

Thus the companions' virtue shines in acts of omission, and what they do not tell in their stories is another confirmation that their report is at peace when reunited with that covering letter.

Since the ultra-elucidating *Letter of Presentation* opens our narrative — thanks to Fr. Cambell and Mrs. Brooke — no further words are needed to describe the work being introduced in this *Introduction*. The letter takes care of that quite well, as it should.

The narrative is endowed with a singular kind of value because its use had been entrusted to the Minister General's discretion. The task of the companions was restricted to the preparing of the information they wanted him to have. They were not hampered by the concern for literary proprieties and the discreet attention to tactfulness and prudence which would have been the duty of an author writing a *legenda* for the edification and safe guidance of friars and faithful. They simply wrote what they wanted their superior to know, and what they had to tell him has weathered the centuries and has been spared for us.

We may therefore expect to sense unusual freshness and candor in the companions' stories, and if we will be patient with the thought patterns of another age, have the joy of discovering new lights on the question: *Who was St. Francis?* (¹).

SALVATOR BUTLER O.F.M.
Convento San Damiano, Assisi

(¹) Academic investigation of the claims made for this book are foreign to the purpose for which it was prepared. One could begin such

The series of stories published in this book has been translated from the Latin text as established in the volume of Fr. Jacques Cambell entitled *I fiori dei tre compagni* (see note p. XVII).

Three Companions of St. Francis, Brothers Leo, Rufinus, and Angelus, claim responsibility for the narrative, that is, of the material reported. They have the attitude of assenting with one mind to the affirmations, and by expressing the hope that eventually their material will be taken in hand by a professional writer, signify that they made no issue of who did the actual writing of the manuscript. Nevertheless, the question has arisen of whether one of the three did all the actual writing of the many reports, or most of it, along with the further question of which one would have been that writer. Answers to these questions could have important repercussions within the general field of Franciscanism. For the appreciation of the present narrative, it is sufficient to recognize the sincerity of whoever contributed the information. I therefore refer to the authority of three men claiming they were with St. Francis, and speak of authors in the plural.

---

a study, should he so desire, by consulting, for instance, the *Introduction* of Fr. THÉOPHILE DESBONNETS O.F.M., to the *Legend of Perugia* in *St. Francis of Assisi - Omnibus of Sources* (Franciscan Herald Press, 1972); ROSALIND B. BROOKE, *The Writings of Leo, Rufino, and Angelo, Companions of St. Francis* (Oxford Medieval Texts, Oxford, 1970); and Fr. JACQUES CAMBELL O.F.M., *I fiori dei tre compagni* (Vita e Pensiero, Milano, 1967).

The authors did not excel in the art of literary craftsmanship, nor in the mastery of Latin, even the medieval Latin of their day. I have given prior attention to stating accurately what these men intended to tell rather than reproducing in English the words they used to tell it. For the sake of smooth reading, I have straightened out some tangled sentences, and in rare instances have recast a paragraph when the sequence was clearly jumbled.

I have adopted the order of the stories which Fr. Cambell established as approximating the order followed in the original text of the companions. It may safely be assumed that the narrative had not been developed according to a well-defined plan in the beginning. Although different scholars have important reasons for holding different views on the original order, no-one can as yet be certain of restoring whatever sequence was observed in the manuscript delivered to Brother Crescentius in 1246.

From the practical point of view, the reader could logically begin or finish his reading at one point as well as another. However, running throughout the narrative like threads are a number of key themes that can be discerned as uppermost in the concerns of the authors. Consequently they are likely to be guidelines to the more important traits of St. Francis, and to the understanding of his motivations and aims. A list of headings indicating such themes has been drawn up alphabetically in the form of a topical index and placed at the back of this book. The reader could devise his own order for usage of the book by pursuing the themes of interest to him with the help of the references noted in that index.

Brother, brothers: These words translate *frater* and *fratres,* in modern parlance, *friars.* The writers retained the warmth, strength and intimacy of natural family ties when using these words with reference to fellows in religion, comprising priests and superiors.

Lesser Brothers: This term is used as a more or less apt translation of *Fratres Minores,* in other words, *Friars Minor.* The gospel sense of "the least of these" (*Mt* 25; 40,45) was accepted at face value by the companions.

Order: In the narration the word *religio,* that is, *religion,* was used to signify what is now designated as a religious *Order.*

Place: This word is the equivalent of the Latin *locus* frequently used in the text to designate a dwelling of the brothers. The authors' term is vague; so must the translator's be, and the reader will have to be left wondering what size, shape and organization the building or buildings in question had. Whatever the structures may have been, one may understand that they were rude, not built for comfort, but rather as a shelter for men thinking of God's Kingdom in terms of permanent abode.

WE WERE WITH
ST. FRANCIS

LETTER OF PRESENTATION

To the Reverend father in Christ, Brother Crescentius,

by the grace of God, Minister General, Brother Leo, Brother Rufinus and Brother Angelus, formerly companions, although unworthy, of the most blessed father Francis, give due and devout reverence in the Lord.

The latest General Chapter and yourself have ordered that the brothers are required to report to your Paternity signs· and miracles of the most blessed father Francis which they know, or about which they may obtain knowledge. Therefore, it has seemed good to us, who, although unworthy, dealt with him for a long time, to impart to your Holiness, with truth guiding, a few of his many acts either witnessed by us or learnt from other holy brothers. These are especially Brother Philip, Visitor of the Poor Ladies, Brother Illuminatus of Arce, Brother Masseus of Marignano, Brother John, companion of the venerable Brother Giles, who got a number of the stories from Brother Giles, and Brother Bernard of sacred memory, the first companion of St. Francis.

We were not satisfied with narrating his sole miracles, for indeed they do not make, but make manifest holiness, but have been moved by the desire to make known deeds illustrative of his holy activities and his will regarding pious endeavor, and thus give praise and glory to the most high God and the same most holy Father, and edification to those who want to follow in his footsteps.

We have not written these things in the form of a biographical story, for such writings on his life and the miracles the Lord worked through him have already been composed. Rather, we have gathered, as from a lovely field, what in our mind were the most beautiful flowers, without following an historical sequence. We have studiously omitted many things that have already been recorded with as great truthfulness as literary brilliance in the aforesaid biographies. If in your discretion it seems fitting, you could have our few reports inserted among them.

We believe that if the venerable men who composed the said biographical stories had been acquainted with the matters we recount, they would by no means have ignored them, but would have adorned at least some part of them with literary expression and left them to be remembered by posterity.

We wish your holy Paternity all prosperity in the Lord Jesus Christ, in whom we, your devoted sons, humbly and devoutly recommend ourselves to your Holiness.

Given at the place at Greccio, August 11, the year of the Lord 1246.

St. Francis nearing death is brought to Assisi

To safeguard their future relic the Assisans send soldiers to bring back St. Francis — the soldiers learn the excellence of begging.

When St. Francis returned from Siena and the Celle of Cortona, he first came to the church of St. Mary of the Portiuncula, and then went to stay a while in the place at Bagnara, above Nocera. Some brothers were living there in a house which had recently been built for them. He stayed there for some time. Already his feet and legs had begun to swell up from his dropsy, and while he was up there his condition became extremely serious.

When the people of Assisi heard about how ill he was at Bagnara they sent some soldiers with all speed to fetch him back to Assisi. They feared he might die there and people of some other city would get possession of his most holy body.

While bringing back the ailing St. Francis, they stopped to rest and eat in a castle town within the Assisi township. St. Francis and his companions went for their rest to the house of a man who had gladly and very warmly offered them hospitality.

In the meantime the soldiers went about the town looking for some food to buy, but they could not find anything. They came back to St. Francis and in a jesting way remarked, "Brother, you will have to give us some of your alms. There is nothing to buy in the town." In a transport of the spirit St. Francis said, "I'll tell you why you couldn't find anything. You trusted your flies — he meant their money — and were not trusting in God. Now go back to the houses where you tried to buy food and see to it that you are not ashamed. This time ask the people to give you alms for the love of God. The Holy Spirit will inspire them. You will get what you want, and plenty of it."

So they went and begged alms as the holy Father had told them to do, and the men and women very cheerfully and very generously shared with them what they had. The soldiers came back happy and joyful to St. Francis and told him what had happened. In their opinion this was a true miracle because they had seen verified to the letter what the holy Father had foretold.

God's love justifies begging

How begging is enobled — for the love of the Son
God gives us all we have in alms — an alms-giver
can make an excellent bargain — St. Francis is true
to Lady Poverty and his vow.

In the mind of St. Francis, begging alms for the
love of the Lord God was a very noble, worthy
and gentlemanly thing to do, both in the eyes
of God and according to worldly judgment. He reasoned
that after mankind had fallen into sin, all the things the
heavenly Father had created for man's use were given to
both worthy and unworthy men gratuitously as alms,
because of his love for his beloved Son. So, as St. Francis
used to say, a servant of God should beg alms for the
love of the Lord more willingly and gladly than a courtly
gentleman taking pleasure in his generosity. In making
a purchase he says, "Give me this penny's worth of goods
and I shall give you a hundred pieces of silver for it."
The servant of God gives a thousandfold more than he
receives because what he offers is the love of God, and
this is what a man gains in return for the alms he gives.
Compared to God's love, all things on earth are as nothing — and even the things of heaven.

Before the brothers had begun to increase in numbers,
and also after they had become numerous, St. Francis
would journey about preaching. He went to preach in
many cities and castle towns where the brothers did not
yet have places. Sometimes a wealthy nobleman would

invite him reverently to accept his hospitality and dine with him in his home. Even though the holy Father knew that his host had prepared plentifully for his bodily needs, he would go begging at mealtime so as to assure a good example for the brothers, and so as to honor the nobility and dignity of Lady Poverty.

It was a usual thing for him to say to his host, "I won't renounce my royal dignity, my heritage, my vocation, and the vows I and the other Lesser Brothers have made. I'm going out and beg for alms. It may be that I'll come back with no more than a few scraps, but I shall have fulfilled my duty." Thus, against the wishes of his host, he would go out begging, and the host would go along with him. On returning, his host would take the alms that had been given to St. Francis and keep them, cherishing them as relics. The one who writes this has often seen such things happen and gives testimony thereto.

St. Francis is a guest of the Lord Bishop of Ostia

Distinguished guests show pious reverence to Francis the beggar — St. Francis honors both the pope's delegate and his royal privilege of poverty — he will be an example of joy in poverty for the sake of his brothers.

Once while visiting the Lord Bishop of Ostia, who later became pope, he went out at mealtime to beg. Out of respect for the Lord Bishop, he went out secretly. When he returned, the Lord Bishop was already seated at table and had begun to eat, for he had guests with him, some knights who were his relatives. St. Francis put the food he had begged on the table of the Lord Bishop and took his place at his side. The Lord Bishop wanted St. Francis to be seated beside him at mealtime whenever he stayed with him.

The Lord Bishop was uncomfortably embarrassed by St. Francis's begging, but he refrained from remarking about it before the guests. After he had eaten a little, St. Francis took some of the food he had begged and offered a little of it in the name of the Lord God to each one of the knights and chaplains. All alike received it with reverence. Some ate it, others kept it as an article of devotion. Indeed, they uncovered their heads in accepting it as a gesture of reverence for St. Francis. The Lord Bishop was very glad to see their pious behavior, especially because the bread was coarse and not wheat bread.

After dinner, the Lord Bishop got up and went to his chamber, taking St. Francis along with him. Exulting and overcome with joy, he stretched out his arms and embraced St. Francis. He said, "Oh why, brother, my simpleton, did you want to shame me by going out to beg while you were a guest in my house, the house of your brothers?"

St. Francis replied, "Lord, in doing what I did, I was actually showing you great honor. When a subject carries out and fulfills his office in obedience to his lord, he honors that lord and superior." He went on to say, "It is my obligation to be a model and example for your poor men. I am aware that there are Lesser Brothers living the life of the Order now, as there will be in days to come, in name and in deed. Because of their love of the Lord God, and the unction of the Holy Spirit who teaches and will continue to teach them all things, they lower themselves and become truly humble; they subject themselves to their brothers, and serve them. But there are now, and will be in the future, some brothers who allow themselves to be deterred by a sense of shame or by lax customs. They disdain to lower themselves and refuse to go humbly and beg alms or do any servile kind of work.

"It is therefore my duty to teach by my actions the men now in the Order, as well as those who will be in it in future times, so that they will be without excuse before God in this world or in the next.

"You, our lord and ruler in the pope's name, are ranked among the great and the rich in the eyes of the world. It is without doubt for the love of God that you and other exalted personages receive me into your houses, and even coerce me into coming. Nevertheless, when I'm staying in your house, I don't want to be ashamed to go and beg alms. Indeed, I want to remain true to my belief that when I beg I do something very noble, am acting with royal dignity, and honoring the all-highest King, who although lord of all things, for our sake made himself the servant of all, and although rich and glorious in his majesty, came among us in our humanity, poor and despised.

"It is therefore my will to make known to those

who are and will be my brothers that I consider it a greater joy of soul and body to sit at the poor table of the brothers, where I see before me the wretched alms they have begged from door to door for love of the Lord God, than when I sit at your table, or at the table of other lords, set with food in abundance and variety, and which is offered me in a spirit of reverence.

"Begged bread is holy bread. It is sanctified by the praise and the love of God. When a brother goes to beg alms, he first says, 'May the Lord God be praised and blessed!' and then, 'Give us alms for the love of the Lord God.'"

The Lord Bishop was greatly edified by St. Francis's words, and he said, "Son, do what is good in your eyes, because the Lord is with you, and you with him!"

The companions are taught to beg

Brothers of distinguished family also begged — idleness is the sign of a fleshly-minded man — the Saint's joy in the happy beggar.

I t was St. Francis's will, as he frequently stated, that a brother should not let much time pass without going out to beg. Otherwise he might become ashamed of the practice. As a matter of fact, the more a brother had been noble and of high standing in the world, the more it would edify him and gladden him to go begging and do servile works for the giving of good example. This is the way things were in the early days.

When the Order was just beginning, and the brothers were living at Rivotorto, there was one of the brothers who prayed little, did no work, and would not go to beg because it made him feel ashamed — but he ate well. In considering his case, St. Francis knew through the Holy Spirit that he was a fleshly-minded man. He told him, "Go your way, Brother Fly. What you want is to eat what your brothers labor for, and you want to pass your time idle instead of doing works of God. You're like Brother Drone who won't work and produce, but eats what the good bees work for and produce." So, that man went his way, and like the fleshly-minded man he was, did not ask forgiveness.

Another time, a spiritual man at the church of St. Mary of the Angels returned with alms on a day when St. Francis was staying there. As he came down the road alongside the church, he began praising God happily and in a loud voice. St. Francis heard him and went out on the road. He rushed up to him, and joyfully kissed the shoulder on which he carried his sackful of alms. He took the sack from his shoulder, put it on his own, and carried it into the brothers' house. In there he stood before the brothers and said, "This is the way I want to see a brother of mine go begging. He goes out and comes back happily and joyfully because of the alms he gets!"

St. Francis at the bishop's palace

The Assisans place their Saint under guard while awaiting his body as a venerable relic — the singing of the *Canticle* turns suffering into joyous praise — pastoral concern for the guards' edification — an answer to the prudent Brother Elias — St. Francis is moved to declare his union with his Lord.

I n those days when St. Francis had returned from the place at Bagnara, he stayed in the bishop's palace where he lay extremely ill. The people of Assisi were afraid he was going to die during the night without their knowing about it, and that the brothers would take his body away secretly and have it kept in some other city. They took action and decided to have men stand guard every night around the walls of the bishop's palace.

Even though St. Francis was very seriously ill, he would often have his companions sing the *Praises of the Lord* during the day. These were the *Praises* he had composed during his illness a while before. He did this to cheer his spirit, lest it should fail him in the trials of his great and many ailments. He would also have them sung at nighttime when, he thought, it would edify the men standing guard outside the palace.

Brother Elias became concerned with St. Francis's manner of comforting and cheering himself and rejoicing in the Lord when he was in such an advanced state of illness. One day he had a talk with him and said, " My dear brother, for me it is a great consolation and source of edification to find you showing yourself so happy for your own and your companions' sake. On the other hand, the people of this city, who indeed deem you, living or dead, a saint, are convinced that you are gravely and incurably ill and are going to die very soon. When they hear you singing your *Canticle* so happily, they could wonder about it and start talking. They could remark to one another, 'That man is about to die — how is this that he can make such a show of gaiety ? He ought to be thinking about death.'"

St. Francis replied, "Do you remember the vision you saw at Foligno ? Weren't you told by someone that I would not live more than another two years ? Even before you saw that vision, by the grace of the Holy Spirit, who suggests all things to our minds, and gives utterance to them in our speech, I had frequently meditated, day and night, upon my end. From the hour you saw that vision I have been even more careful to meditate upon the hour of my death."

Then in a transport of the spirit he said, "Brother, let me be happy in the Lord and rejoice in singing my *Praises* to him while I am suffering my illness, because, by the grace of God and the help of the Holy Spirit, I am so closely united and at one with my Lord that by his mercy I have good reason to rejoice in Him, the All-highest."

St. Francis is informed of his imminent death

An example of the Saint's literal acceptance of gospel teaching — he insists upon a frank statement on his health — a welcome to Sister Death.

In those days on another occasion, a doctor whose name was Bonus Johannes (Good John), of the city of Arezzo, well known to St. Francis, and a friend of his, came to visit him in that place. St. Francis questioned him on his illness. He said, "How do you find my dropsy, Finiatu?"

If a man had the name of Bonus (Good), St. Francis would not pronounce his name because of due reverence to the Lord who said, "None is good but God alone (*Lk* 18,19)." Likewise, he would not call anyone *father* or *master*, nor use these terms in writing letters because of reverence for the Lord who said, "Only one is your father; the One in heaven," and "Only one is your master, etc. (*Mt* 23,9,10)."

The doctor told him, "Brother, you will get along alright by the grace of the Lord." He did not want to tell him he was going to die soon. St. Francis questioned him again: "Tell me the truth, what to you really think? Don't be afraid; by the grace of God I am not faint-hearted, and I am not afraid to die. With the Lord's help and by his mercy and grace, I am so closely united and at one with my Lord that I am as pleased to die as I am to live, and vice versa."

Then the doctor told him clearly, "Father, according to our medical science your illness cannot be cured, and you will either die at the end of September or the fourth of October."

St. Francis, who was lying ill in bed, spread out his arms and hands, and with all devotion and reverence for God, and rejoicing inwardly and outwardly said, "Sister Death, I welcome you!"

St. Francis declares his intentions on the rule

In view of controversy among the brothers on interpretation of the rule, Brother Richer secures a statement from St. Francis.

Brother Richer was a brother whom St. Francis held in warm affection. He was from the March of Ancona, and of noble family, but was still nobler for his sanctity. He came one day to visit St. Francis at that place. There he spoke to him about various matters concerning the Order and the observation of the rule. He questioned him on a particular point, saying, "Tell me, Father, what intention you had in mind at the beginning of the Order when you had just begun to have brothers, and what intention you have now, and expect to keep until the day of your death? I want to be able to know with certainty what your first and your final intention is. Tell me then: May we brothers who

16

are clerics and have a number of books keep those books under the condition that we say they are property of the Order?" St. Francis replied, "I tell you, brother, that this was and is my first and last intention as it is my will, and may the brothers put credence in my words, that none of the brothers should have anything excepting his tunic, as conceded by the rule, with a cord, and breeches."

The little flock

St. Francis explains humility and poverty as means to the possession of Christ — a gospel source for the name *Fratres Minores* — the name becomes official.

Sometimes St. Francis would say, "The rule and life of the Lesser Brothers is like a little last hour flock. The Son has asked his heavenly Father for it, saying, 'Father, I would like you to form and give me a new and humble people in this last hour. Let them be different in humility and poverty from any that ever existed before, and may they be content in having only me.' The Father said to his beloved Son, 'My Son, what you have asked has been done.'"

St. Francis would say that it was for this reason that the Lord wished them to be called *Lesser Brothers*, for they are the people whom the Son of God requested of his Father. The Son of God says of them in the Gospel,

"Do not fear, little flock. It has pleased your Father to give you the kingdom." And again, "I assure you, as often as you did it for one of my least brothers, you did it for me (*Lk* 12,32; *Mt* 25,40)." Of course, it is understood that the Lord was speaking of all men who are poor in spirit, but primarily he was foretelling the coming of the Order of Lesser Brothers into the Church.

Since it was revealed to St. Francis that the Order should be called of the *Lesser Brothers* (*Fratrum Minorum*), he had that name written in the first rule when he submitted it to the Lord Pope Innocent III, who approved it and conceded it, and then proclaimed it to all in Council.

St. Francis teaches the brothers a salutation

A form of salutation is required by reason of a divine inspiration — a brother should use it in spite of embarrassment — a further statement on St. Francis's basic motive for poverty.

In like manner the Lord revealed to him the greeting that the brothers should use. It is written in his *Testament* where it is said, "*The Lord revealed to me* that I should say as greeting: 'May the Lord give you peace!'" At the beginning of the Order St. Francis went out one time with a brother who was one of the first twelve brothers. He greeted any men and women they met along the road or saw in the fields with the words, "May the Lord give you peace!" This was a greeting the people had never heard any Religious use before, and they were astonished. Some became indignant. They asked, "What do you mean by using such a greeting as this?" The brother was left very embarrassed. He spoke to St. Francis about it and said, "Brother, let me use some other greeting." St. Francis answered, "Let them talk. They cannot be expected to understand the things of God. Don't let it embarrass you. I tell you, brother, even noblemen and princes of the world are going to show reverence to you and the other brothers because you greet them in this way."

The Lord wanted a people who want only him

Again St. Francis's cherished motive for poverty is reported.

St. Francis also said, "Isn't it a grand thing that the Lord wanted to have a little people who more than all those who had preceded would be happy having nothing at all but his most high and glorious Self!"

The companions add their testimony
to Brother Richer's

Witness to the Saint's declaration of his intentions on
the rule — explanation of his tolerance of more lenient
practice — greater motive for his own exemplary observance — a response on the possession of books — a
colorful reproof — opposing Ministers oppose God's
will.

Let no brother ever assert that in his time St.
Francis did not have the brothers observe, and
did not command them to observe such strict
poverty as Brother Richer reports. We who were with
St. Francis would have a response for such a brother.
We have heard him tell the brothers the very same thing
and more, and had many such things written in the rule.
In fact in assiduous prayer and meditation he had de-
manded these things of the Lord for the good of the
Order, and declared them absolutely the will of the Lord.
But later when he made them known to the brothers,
they thought such obligations would be burdensome and
insupportable, especially in view of the fact that they
could not then know what the future of the Order would
be after the Saint's death.

Since he greatly feared arousing anger and antagonism
within himself and in the brothers, he did not want to
contend with them. He gave way, although reluctantly,
to their will and excused himself before the Lord. So that
the words the Lord had placed in his mouth for the good
of the brothers should not return to him empty, he

wanted them to be fulfilled in his own person, and in this way gain the Lord's reward. With this solution his spirit was put to rest and consoled until the end.

One time when he had returned from overseas, a certain Minister spoke to him about the chapter on poverty. He wanted to know what St. Francis's will was on this issue, and what his understanding was regarding a statement written in the rule about things prohibited by the Holy Gospel, namely, " Take nothing for the way, etc. (*Lk* 9,3). " St. Francis answered, " I want it to be understood in the sense that the brothers must have nothing excepting a tunic with a cord, and breeches, as the rule states. When obliged by necessity, they may have footwear. "

The Minister then said, " What then should I do ? I have a number of books and they are worth more than fifty libras. " He said this because he wanted to keep them with an easy conscience. His conscience was troubled because he had so many books, and was aware of St. Francis's strict understanding of the chapter on poverty.

St. Francis replied, " Brother, I neither can nor should go counter to my conscience and the observance of the Holy Gospel we have vowed. "

The Minister was saddened to hear these words. St. Francis saw that he was perturbed, and in a transport of the Spirit told him, as if to the personification of all the brothers, " You Lesser Brothers want to appear as observers of the Holy Gospel in the eyes of men, and have them call you such, but by your deeds you proclaim that what you want is coffers! "

The Ministers knew very well that they were bound by the rule to observe the Holy Gospel. Notwithstanding, they had the chapter deleted from the rule where it was said, " Take nothing for the way. " They did not believe they were bound to observe Holy Gospel perfection.

St. Francis was enlightened by the Holy Spirit to know this. He declared before some of the brothers, " Do the Ministers think they can deceive both God and me ? " He also said, " Indeed, so that all the brothers may know and be aware that they are bound to observe Holy Gospel perfection, I want it to be written both at the beginning and the end of the rule that the brothers are bound to observe *the Holy Gospel of our Lord Jesus Christ*. Lest the brothers have any excuse before God, I will proclaim by my deeds, and with the help of the Lord, I will persevere to the end in observing the things the Lord placed in my mouth for the salvation and the good of my own and the brothers' souls, and which I have in the past and do now announce to them. "

He therefore observed the Holy Gospel to the letter. He did this from the very beginning when he began to have brothers until the day of his death.

The dangers of learning

A novice's request to have a book — the ways of sanctification that are sure — learning and books not for his
brothers even though the theologically learned are to
be revered — spiritual fervor is lost even through study
of Scripture — learned preachers pride themselves on
fruits granted because of works done in silence by the
Saint's Knights of the Round Table — why holy men
are kept ignorant of their apostolic achievements —
dignity of office and pastoral occupations do not exempt
from prayer and menial tasks — the response to the
novice is vividly illustrated.

At one time there was a novice who could read
the Psalter, but not very well. Since he liked to
read it, he requested permission from the Minister General to have a Psalter, and the Minister granted
his request. However, the brother did not want to have
it unless he would first get permission from St. Francis,
for he had heard that the holy Father did not want his
brothers to have any desire for learning and books. Rather,
as he already knew, St. Francis had expressed his will
to the brothers in his preaching. They should strive to
possess and imitate pure and holy simplicity, holy prayer,
and Lady Poverty, the same means the first brothers had
used to achieve their sanctification. He believed this to
be the surer way to follow for the salvation of their souls.

Yet he did not scorn or despise holy learning; rather
he held in affection and reverence the learned men of
the Order, as he did all learned men. He testifies to this

23

in his *Testament* where he says, "We should honor and venerate all theologians and those who administer divine teaching, for they administer spirit and life to us."

However, in looking toward the future, he knew by the Holy Spirit, as he frequently remarked to the brothers, that there would be many brothers who in their work of edifying others would lose their own vocation, namely pure and holy simplicity, holy prayer, and our Lady Poverty. Those brothers who had become convinced that a knowledge of Scripture would imbue them more fully with devotion and love of God, would through their study of it become spiritually frigid. They would be as if empty internally.

Such brothers would never be able to recover their former vocation because they would never have time to live according to their vocation. As he said, "I fear that what they appear to possess will be taken from them because they will have forsaken their vocation."

He also said, "There are many who busy themselves solely with advancing their learning and are concerned with that and that only. If they preach to the people and then learn that some of them have been edified or converted to penitence, they get puffed up, or they flatter themselves because of the works which actually others have done. Because of the prayers of the holy brothers, the Lord had done the work of edifying and converting to penitence which these men think they had done by their words. Those holy brothers don't know what they have accomplished, because it is God's will that they remain unaware of it, lest they become proud. These are

24

my *Knights of the Round Table!* They are the brothers who go and hide themselves in the wilderness or in secluded places so that they can give themselves the more assiduously to prayer, and weep for their own sins and the sins of others.

"Their holiness is known by God, and often is not recognized by their brothers or by the people. But when the angels present them to the Lord, then the Lord will display to them the fruit and the recompense of their labors in the many souls they have saved by their prayers, and he will say to them, 'My sons, see the souls you have saved by your prayers', and 'because you were faithful in little things, I shall make you ruler over many' (*Mk* 25,23)."

In this regard, St. Francis would comment on the passage: "The barren woman has borne many, and she who had many sons has waned (cf. *I Sam* 2,5)." The good religious was like the barren woman who edifies himself and others with his holy works and virtues. He would frequently repeat this when giving talks to the brothers, and in particular at a Chapter held at the church of St. Mary of the Portiuncula when addressing the Ministers and the other brothers.

In explaining the nature of work to all the brothers, including Ministers and preachers, he told them that whatever the dignity of their office, or the duties involved in their preaching, they must on no account neglect holy and devout prayer, begging alms, and working with their hands like the other brothers, for the sake of giving good example and for the profit of their own and others' souls.

He also said, " The brothers who are subjects are greatly edified when their Ministers and the preachers willingly retire to pray, and when they demean and humble themselves. "

He himself, as a faithful and zealous servant of Christ, practiced what he taught his brothers for as long as his health permitted.

The brother novice mentioned above was staying in a certain hermitage when St. Francis happened to come there. In a talk he had with the holy Father, the brother said, " Father, I would like very much to have a Psalter. The Minister has given his permission for it, but still I won't have it without your consent. "

By way of reply, St. Francis said, " The Emperor Charles, Roland and Oliver, and other great heroes, strong men, and mighty in battle, pursued the infidels with sweat and toil unto death. Their victory over them was glorious and memorable. At the end, these holy martyrs died in combat for the faith of Christ. But many are the men who expect people to shower honor and praise upon them for the mere retelling of what those great men did. "

So as to affirm this teaching, he clarified the meaning of his words in the *Admonitions* where he says, " The Saints did the deeds, and we in the telling and the preaching about them want to reap the honor and the glory. " He also said, " Learning puffs up, but charity builds up. "

Another time, St. Francis was sitting by the fire warming himself. The same brother spoke to him about the Psalter again. St. Francis told him, "When you get a Psalter, you will start to yearn for a Breviary. When you get a Breviary, you will enthrone yourself on a chair like a grand prelate and say to your brother, 'Bring me my Breviary.'" After saying this, his spirit was transported. He took a handful of ashes and poured them on his head while crying out as if to himself, "I want a Breviary! I want a Breviary!" Over and over he poured ashes on his head and rubbed them in, while repeating these words. The brother sat dumbfounded and was reduced to shame.

Finally St. Francis said to him, "Brother, I too was once tempted like you are to have books. So as to know what the Lord's will was, I took a book in which the gospels of the Lord were written, and I prayed to the Lord and I asked Him that he deign to show me his will on the matter with the first opening of the book. I finished praying and I opened the book. The first words my eyes fell upon was this passage: 'To you it has been given to know the mystery of the Kingdom of God. To those outsiders it is announced in parables (*Mk* 4,11).'"

He also said, "Many are the men who gladly climb to the heights of learning, but blessed is the man who makes himself barren for the love of the Lord God."

27

Again the brother wanting a book

By word and action the Saint eradicates a mistake — holy deeds are the measure of merit.

After some months had passed, St. Francis was staying at the church of St. Mary of the Portiuncula. He was standing in the road near the cell behind the house when that same brother spoke to him again about the Psalter. St. Francis said, "Go and do what your Minister said you could." On hearing this, the brother turned and went back along the road toward the place from which he had come. St. Francis stood where he was on the road. He started thinking about what he had told the brother. Suddenly he called to him and said, "Wait for me, brother, wait!" Then he walked up to him and said, "Come back with me, brother, and show me the spot where I stood when I told you to do what your Minister said."

When they were back at that same place, St. Francis knelt and bowed before the brother. He said, "My fault, brother, my fault. Anyone wanting to be a Lesser Brother must have nothing else but his tunic, as the rule grants, a cord, and breeches. When the brothers are clearly obliged to it by necessity or illness they may have footwear."

Thereafter he gave this response to any brother who asked his counsel on matters of the sort. In this regard he would say, "A man's learning is measured by his deeds, and a religious is a good preacher insofar as he does good works." In other words, "A tree is known by its fruit (*Lk* 6,44)."

St. Francis explains his toleration of aberrations and his resignation

The brothers' early life remains the norm and most efficacious way of apostolate — even in bad health he could have governed willing brothers — harsh coercion is unbefitting a spiritual vocation — demons will punish transgressors of the Lord's commands — his will on poor buildings — learning is poor authority before God's will.

On another occasion when St. Francis was staying in the bishop's palace at Assisi, one of the companions present said to him, "Father, excuse me please, but what I want to say is what a number of brothers have been thinking about." He then continued, "You know that there was a time when by the grace of God the whole Order thrived in the purity of its perfection. All the brothers observed holy poverty fervently and conscientiously in all they did. Their buildings were small, and they were poor; articles needed for their use were few and poor; they had few books and they were poor, and so was their clothing. In these things, and in other external things, they were all of one will. They took pains to observe whatever had to do with our

29

vows and vocation, and the giving of good example. They were of one mind in loving God and neighbor.

"However, for a while now, this pure kind of perfection has been changing and becoming different. A lot of discussion is being done, and the brothers are making the excuse that now that they have become numerous such things can no longer be observed. Moreover, there are many brothers who are convinced that the people are more edified by their own idea of our way than the one I first mentioned. On this account they have formed the opinion that there is greater virtue in living and acting in this different way. As consequence, it is now their mind that the way of simplicity and our former poverty which gave rise to our Order, and which were its foundations, are matters of no account.

"We have given serious consideration to these changes, and we are convinced that they are not to your liking. We wonder then why you tolerate them and do nothing to correct them."

St. Francis made this reply: "May the Lord forgive you, brother, for opposing me and taking a stand against me. You want to get me involved in things not within my competence." He went on to explain, "As long as I held the office of governing the brothers and they remained true to their vocation and their vows, even though I was a feeble man from the beginning of my conversion to Christ, I was able to govern them satisfactorily with minimum attention. My example and preaching were enough.

"As time went on, I saw how the Lord was daily

30

increasing the number of brothers. Because of tepidity and dearth of spiritual life, they began to veer away from the straight and sure way we were used to following, and as you have said, chose to go by a broader way. They became heedless of their vows, their vocation, and the giving of good example, nor would they respond to my preaching and example and give up the way they had started to follow. It was then that I confided the Order of the brothers to the Lord and the Ministers.

"Indeed, at the moment of my renunciation and retirement from office in the government of the brothers, I excused myself before them at the General Chapter on the grounds that illness prevented me from assuming responsibility for their care and welfare. Nevertheless if they wanted to proceed, and if they had been proceeding according to my will, then for their encouragement, I would not wish them to have any Minister excepting myself until the day of my death.

"A faithful and good subject knows and observes the will of his superior, and does not need much attention. Indeed, I would be so glad of such a brother's goodness, and so encouraged by the reward he and I too were gaining, that even while lying ill in bed, it would be no burden to me to give him all the attention he needed."

He went on to say, "My office is a spiritual one, I mean the government of the brothers. I must overcome and correct vices. If I cannot do this by means of my preaching and example, then I would not want to become a brutish tyrant and beat and flog the brothers as a worldly kind of master does.

31

"I place my trust in the Lord. We are assailed by invisible enemies who are the Lord's police force in this world and the next for punishing those who transgress God's commandments. They will duly punish transgressors; they will see to it that the transgressing brothers are corrected at the hand of the men of this world who will scorn them and work their disgrace. This is the way they will be recalled to their vows and vocation.

"I tell you truly that until the day of my death I shall not cease teaching the brothers by my example and actions how to walk in the way the Lord has shown me. I have shown it to them, and have so taught them that they are without excuse before the Lord. Before God I do not hold myself accountable for anything further between me and them."

Consequently he had it written in his *Testament* that all the brothers' houses were to be built with clay and timbers as a sign of holy poverty and humility, and that the churches built for the brothers should be small. In fact he wanted a reform to be carried out with regard to houses built from timbers and clay and all other good examples. It should begin at the place of St. Mary of the Portiuncula. This was the place, after the brothers had begun to live there, where the Lord first began to multiply their numbers. He intended that it should remain always a model and memorial for the other brothers, both those then in the Order and those who would later enter it.

However, there were brothers who told him it did not seem a good thing to them that they all be obliged to build from clay and timbers, for the reason that wood was more expensive than stone in many places and provinces. St. Francis did not want to oppose them because he was extremely ill and near to death; in fact he lived for only a short time afterwards. But following upon this discussion he wrote in his *Testament:* "Let the brothers take care that they firmly refuse to accept churches and dwellings and all other things built for them unless they be worthy of the holy poverty we have promised in the rule, and where they always sojourn like strangers and pilgrims."

We who were with him when he wrote the rule and practically all his other writings, testify that he had many things written in the rule and in his other writings which were opposed by some of the brothers, especially the superiors. It has turned out that those things in which the brothers opposed St. Francis during his life, would now, after his death, be very beneficial to the whole Order.

It was because he greatly feared arousing anger and antagonism that he ceded, although unwillingly, to the will of the brothers. But often he would make this statement: "Woe to those brothers who oppose me in matters which I know to be God's will, for the greater good of the Order, even if I do cede reluctantly to their will."

He would often remark to his companions, "In this is my grief and my affliction: I obtain from God in his mercy things which are for the good of the whole Order at the present time and in the future, at the price of strenuous labor of prayer and meditation, and am assured by him that they conform to his will. And yet some brothers who have no authority or enlightenment except-

ing their learning render them void and stand in opposition to me. They say, 'These things are to be held
and observed, and not those.'" But as has been said, he
so greatly feared arousing their anger and antagonism
that he allowed many things to be done, and ceded to
their will in many things which were not in accord with
his will.

A last supper and a blessing

Expecting to die St. Francis breaks bread with his
companions and blesses them — he intends that the
sharing of bread and the blessing embrace all brothers
to come — the bread has the power of working cures.

One night St. Francis suffered so acutely from the
pains of his illness that he could hardly get any
rest or sleep the whole night. When morning
came, the pains subsided somewhat, and he had all the
brothers then staying in the place called, and had them sit
before him. In looking at them, he saw in them representatives of all the brothers. Beginning with one of the brothers, he blessed each one, placing his right hand on his
head, and then extended his blessing to each single brother
then in the Order, and to all who would enter it until the
end of time. He appeared to regret that he could not see all
his sons and brothers before dying.

Afterwards he ordered that some loaves of bread be
brought before him, and he blessed them. Since he was

34

too ill to break the bread, he had one of the brothers break the loaves into pieces. He took them and handed a piece to each brother telling him to eat the whole thing.

Just as the Lord had wanted to eat with his apostles on a Thursday, so did St. Francis. It seemed to the brothers that he was wanting to bless them and in them all the brothers. In eating that blessed bread, they were to eat as if all the other brothers were eating with them. It is clear that we may hold this opinion for the reason that although the day this happened was not Thursday, he told the brothers he thought it was Thursday.

One of the brothers kept a piece of the bread, and after St. Francis's death some persons who ate a bit of it when ill were immediately cured.

Parsley picked in the dark

It is hard for St. Francis to eat — by virtue of trustful obedience a brother seeks and finds parsley at night.

One night St. Francis was feeling extremely feeble for reason of his grave illness. He said to his companions, "I should like to be comforted a little, brothers. I want to eat something if I can." The companions said, "What do you want to eat, Father?" He said, "If I had some parsley, maybe I could eat a little bread with it." The companions asked the brother who did the cooking, "Brother, do you think you could find some parsley in the garden ? " There was a garden adjoining the palace where St. Francis lay.

The brother answered, "I could hardly find any at night. Even in daytime I wouldn't find any because I have been taking the little there was for everyday use. " St. Francis told him, "Go, brother, maybe you will find some. " The brother answered, "It's very dark tonight, and there is such a strong wind blowing that I can't take a light. How do you expect me to find it ? At night I can't see the plants, and even if it were daytime I couldn't hope to find any!"

St. Francis said, "Go, brother, and don't let it worry you. Just do this: Go into the garden, stoop, and put your hand on the ground. Bring me the first greens you touch. "

The brother went without a light. In the garden he could not tell the difference between weeds and herbs. Simply to satisfy St. Francis, he bent down, picked the first greens he touched, and then brought them in to him.

One of the brothers saw what a bunch of weeds he had and began separating them one from another. Because of St. Francis's faith, by divine dispensation, it happened that he found plenty of fine parsley among the weeds.

This delighted the brothers. They were amazed at this sign of St. Francis's holiness and faith, and they marveled. St. Francis remarked to the companions, "My brothers, when I tell you something to do you should not make me repeat it so often. " He ate a little and felt better for it.

36

So great were the purity and the faith of St. Francis that the Lord rewarded them with both spiritual and bodily miracles for himself and for others. We have seen and known such great and so many miracles worked through him that any of us, if we were to be with him for only a short while, would need a long time to write a report of it all.

St. Francis foresees that his body will be venerated as a relic

A brother makes a joke about a good bargain in stuffs — St. Francis's body will be wrapped in rich silks from Bagdad in exchange for his sackcloth clothing (in medieval times it was a common practice to envelop bodies or relics of saints in costly stuffs imported from Persia, Syria, Byzantium and other eastern countries).

One day, during the time St. Francis lay ill in the bishop's palace at Assisi, one of the brothers, a spiritual and saintly man, jested with him and said laughingly, "When you sell all those pieces of sackcloth to the Lord, how much are you going to get for them ? That skimpy body you have there dressed in sackcloth is going to have stuffs from Bagdad wrapped around it and fine silks layed over it. " At the time St. Francis had a strip of fur wrapped around him because of his illness. This was covered with sackcloth and he

37

was wearing a sackcloth tunic. St. Francis, or rather not he but the Holy Spirit speaking through him, exclaimed in a joyous transport of the spirit, "It's true what you say — it's going to be like that!"

St. Francis satisfies a companion's wish for a relic

The Saint knows his companion's unspoken wish — with a symbolic gesture he makes his habit the possession of the brother.

While St. Francis was in that same palace, one of his companions observed how near to death he seemed to be. He said to himself, "What a wonderful thing for the good of my soul it would be if only I could have my father's tunic after he died!"

A little later St. Francis called him and said, "Take the sleeves of my tunic and hold them in your hands. From now on this is your tunic, and I can't give it to anyone else."

The brother was struck with wonder at such great holiness. He had said no word about it. He had only had the thought in his mind.

St. Francis writes a script for his companion

Answering an unexpressed need St. Francis writes a
holy text for a tempted brother — it acquires miraculous powers.

At a time when St. Francis had retired for solitude
to a cell on Mount Alverna, a companion was
staying there with him. He felt the need of having
in his hands some sort of inspiring script with words
of the Lord written on it. He was being sorely tormented
with an evil temptation, not of the flesh, but of the spirit.
One day St. Francis told him, "Bring me some paper and
ink. I want to write some words of the Lord and some
praises to him which I have been thinking over." The
brother brought them. St. Francis went away and wrote
the words of the *Praises of the Lord* he had in mind. At
the end he added a blessing for the brother. He said,
"Take this script and keep it carefully until the day of
your death."

The brother was overcome with admiration and filled
with joy. Without his asking or saying anything, by the
will of the Lord, the holy Father had fulfilled his desire.

After St. Francis's death, the Lord worked many and
great miracles through that script. Persons with serious
ailments were cured when a sign of the cross was made
over them with that written page.

now: La Verna [handwritten margin note]

St. Francis blesses Assisi

He wills to die at St. Mary of the Angels — he is almost blind — the words of his blessing.

While he was staying in that same palace, St. Francis found his illness was getting worse every day, and had himself carried in a litter to the church of St. Mary of the Portiuncula. He was unable to ride horseback because of the gravity of the condition to which his illness had reduced him.

When the men carrying him were passing along the road alongside the hospital, he told them to set the litter on the ground. Since he could hardly see because of the eye disease that had afflicted him for a long time, he had the litter turned around so that he could face the city of Assisi. He then lifted himself slightly and blessed the city using these words: "O Lord, just as I believe that in former times this was a city where the inhabitants were evil and wicked, and known throughout the country for their infamy, just so do I now see that in your bountiful mercy, when it pleased you to do so, you showed the immensity of your mercies in this place, and have made it become a city inhabited by men who spread the sweet odor of a good life, right doctrine and good fame throughout the whole of the Christian people. I therefore implore you, O Lord Jesus Christ, Father of mercies, not to consider our ingratitude, but keep ever in mind the abundant mercy you have bestowed upon this city. Let it always be one where the inhabitants know you and glorify your blessed and glorious name for ever and ever. Amen."

After he said this, he was carried on to St. Mary of the Portiuncula.

The will to die in absolute poverty

An answer invoked by both action and word — his insistence upon discerning and following the will of the Lord — a mention of the wound in his side — at death he is to be laid naked on the naked ground.

One day St. Francis called his companions to him. When they stood before him, he got out of bed at the cost of a painful effort because of his dropsy and his many other grave ailments, and sat down on the bare ground. His companions had no idea why he was doing this. He took off his clothes, and stayed there naked, sitting on the bare ground. With his left hand he covered the wound in his side so that it would not be seen. Then he spoke; he said, "I have done what I ought to do; now you do what the Lord inspires you to do." He said nothing more, but waited to see what inspiration the Lord would give them.

Indeed from the time of his conversion until the day of his death, in good or bad health, St. Francis took great pains to discern and follow the will of the Lord.

At the sight of him sitting ill and naked on the ground, his companions were overcome with sorrow and pity, and they wept bitterly. One of them, his Guardian, was convinced that the will of the Lord prompted the holy Father to dispossess himself even of the tunic and breeches conceded by the rule so that he would in every way be a poor man of Christ, and his imitator in both life and death.

His Guardian handed the tunic and breeches to him saying, "Father, I give you this tunic and breeches on loan. May it be clear that you have been dispossessed of them because I tell you that you don't have the right to give them to anyone." Raising his eyes heavenward, and joining his hands, St. Francis blessed the Lord, and said to his companions, "May the Lord reward you, because I want to die poor like this."

It was after this that he said to them one day, " As soon as the soul has left my body, take off my clothes and leave me naked, just as I took my clothes off before you, and place me on the bare ground. Let me stay that way for as long as it takes a man to walk a mile."

St. Francis sings a new song because
Sister Death is coming

A brother exhorts the Saint to be exemplary in dying joyfully — Brother Angelus and Brother Leo sing to him his newly composed stanza for the *Canticle* welcoming Sister Death — the words of his new praise to the Lord.

One of the brothers said to St. Francis one day, "Father, your life and your way of acting have been and now are a light and a mirror, not only for your brothers, but for the whole Church of God, just as your death will also be. You may be sure your death will bring immense sorrow and grief to your brothers and many other people too, but for you it will bring enormous consolation and infinite joy. You will pass from strenuous labor to serene rest; from many pains and temptations to infinite happiness; from the drastic poverty you have always loved and willingly borne since the beginning of your conversion until the day of death, to the greatest, the real, and infinite riches; from temporal death to never-ending life where you will see eternally, face to face, the Lord your God whom with so much fervor, desire and love you have contemplated in this world."

After saying this he told him plainly, "Father, you know it is true that unless the Lord send medicine down from heaven for your body, your illness is not to be cured, and you have only a short time to live as the doctors have already declared. I speak to you this way to strengthen your spirit, and so that inwardly and outwardly you will not cease to rejoice in the Lord. Your brothers and other folk coming to visit you know very well that you are about to die. Let them find you rejoicing in the Lord. Let your death be for those who witness it, and for those who will hear about it after you have died, a memorable example, just as your life and way of acting have been. "

Although St. Francis had been brought very low by his illnesses, he praised the Lord, with both the inward and outward man rejoicing, and in a transport of the spirit told the brother, " If I am to die soon, then call Brother Angelus and Brother Leo to me, and have them sing to me about Sister Death. "

Those brothers came to him, and weeping copious tears sang the *Canticle of Brother Sun and the Other Creatures of the Lord*. The Saint had composed this canticle during his illness in praise of the Lord and for the cheering of his own soul and the souls of others. He had placed before the final stanza of this song the verses on Sister Death which are as follows:

Be praised, my Lord
for our sister Bodily Death,
from whom no living man may escape.
Woe to those who die in mortal sin;
blessed are those whom she will find
doing your most holy will,
because the second death will do them no harm.

The arrival of Lady Jacoba

Lady Jacoba receives St. Francis's message without need of his letter — as an exception she is admitted to the enclosure — like the Three Kings she comes with gifts — list of articles brought in preparation for his death.

St. Francis called his companions to him one day and said, " You know how Lady Jacoba of Settesoli has been, and is most faithful and devoted to me and to our Order. I believe that if you would let her know what my condition is she would think it a great favor and kindness.

" Tell her in particular to send you cloth for a tunic. It should be cloth for Religious, the color of ashes, like the cloth the Cistercian monks weave in overseas countries. She should also send some of that pastry she used to make for me when I was at Rome. " The pastry he referred to was called *mortariolum*. It is made of almonds, sugar or honey, and other things.

She was a spiritual woman, a widow, and dedicated to God. Her family was one of the noblest and richest of Rome. She had received great grace from God through the merits and preaching of St. Francis. Like another Magdalen, she spent her time in tears and devout prayer for the love of God.

A letter was written according to the holy Father's words, and a brother had gone to fetch another brother who was to carry the letter to Rome, when suddenly a knock was heard on the door. A brother opened the outer gate and saw before him Lady Jacoba. She had come in all haste from Rome to visit St. Francis. The brother was overjoyed, and rushed back to St. Francis to tell him that Lady Jacoba, with her son and a large company of attendants, had come to visit him. He said, "What shall we do about it, Father ? Are we to let her come in here where you are ?" St. Francis had had a ruling made there in the early days, for the sake of holy decorum and devotion of the place, that no woman should enter that cloister. St. Francis said, "The ruling is not to be observed in the case of this lady who has had great enough faith and devotion to make the journey here from a far away country."

And so she came in to St. Francis and shed tears copiously at his bedside. But a wonderful thing had happened. She had come bringing cloth for the dead, that is ash color, to make a tunic, and all the things the letter asked for. The brothers were overcome with admiration for St. Francis's holiness.

Moreover, Lady Jacoba said to the brothers, "Brothers, while I was in prayer, it was told me in spirit, 'Go and visit your father St. Francis, but quickly and don't delay. If you let any time pass you won't find him alive. Take with you such and such cloth for his tunic, and such and such things to make a certain pastry for him, and take a good quantity of wax for candles, and also some incense.'" St. Francis had not listed incense with the other things in the letter. The Lord had wanted to inspire the lady to bring this additional item for the consolation of her soul and so that we would be made still more aware of the Saint's holiness, for the heavenly Father desired that this poor man be honored on his deathbed. He had inspired kings to come with gifts to honor his beloved Child, his Son, in the days of his birth in poverty. He inspired this noble lady, abiding in a distant country, to come with gifts to venerate and honor the glorious and holy body of his saintly servant, who with burning love loved and followed in life and death the poverty of his beloved Son.

The lady prepared the pastry the holy Father had wanted to eat, but he could take only a very little of it because each day his body was becoming feebler and closer to death. She also had many candles made to be burned around his body after he had departed. The brothers made a tunic from the cloth she had brought, and it was used for his sepulture. He himself told the brothers that they were to sew sackcloth over it in sign and example of most holy humility and poverty.

It so came about that God was pleased to have St. Francis pass away to the Lord during the week in which Lady Jacoba had come.

He had wisely built upon humility and poverty

The Order founded upon poverty and humility —
brothers should serve lepers for humility's sake — various
examples of the Saint's poverty and humility — a
description of his resignation from office as governing
Father of the Order.

From the beginning of his conversion, St. Francis,
with God helping, had like a wise man founded
himself and his house, that is, his Order, upon
firm rock, namely upon the very great humility and the
very great poverty of the Son of God, and he gave his
Order the name of Lesser Brothers.

He built upon very great humility: When the Order
had just begun, after the brothers had commenced to
increase in number he directed the brothers to dwell in
the lepers' hospitals and be at their service; in the time
when both noblemen and men of humble condition were
coming to the Order, he told them, among other things,
that they were expected to serve lepers and stay in their
houses.

He built upon the greatest poverty: As it is stated in
the rule, the brothers should remain "as strangers and
pilgrims" in the houses where they lived, and "want
nothing else under heaven" except holy poverty, through
which they would be nourished by God with food for
the body and with virtues in this world, and which would
be the means of obtaining their heavenly inheritance. He
himself built upon the greatest poverty and humility,

for although he was a distinguished · dignitary in the Church of God, it was his will and choice to remain debased, not only in the Church of God, but among his brothers.

One time when he was preaching to the people of Terni in the square in front of the bishop's palace, the bishop of the city, a man both spiritual and of sound judgment, was present at the sermon. When St. Francis had finished preaching, the bishop arose and said to the people, among other things, "From the time the Lord first planted and built his Church, he has always illuminated it with the light of holy men who cultivated the Church's life with their words and examples. In this last hour," he declared, pointing his finger at St. Francis, "he has illuminated it with this poor, despicable and unlettered man. You are then placed under the obligation of loving and honoring God, and of being on guard against sin. He has not done such things for every nation (*Ps* 147,20)!" When he had finished preaching, the bishop came down from where they had preached and went with St. Francis into the cathedral. In there St. Francis fell down at the bishop's feet, bowed low, and said, " I tell you truly, Lord Bishop, never has a man honored me on this earth as you have honored me today. Other people say, 'This is a holy man!' and ascribe the glory and the holiness to the creature instead of the Creator. But you have separated what is precious from what is worthless, like a man of keen judgment. "

Often when people would honor St. Francis, telling him he was a holy man, he would respond to such speech

49

saying, "I am not yet sure that I won't have sons and daughters!"

Another response was, "If at any moment the Lord should wish to take away from me the treasure he has entrusted to my care, what would there be left for me except a body and soul which is no more than heathens have? Indeed I can only believe that if the Lord had given a thief or even a heathen as many good gifts as he has bestowed upon me, they would be more faithful to the Lord than I am."

He would also say, "Paintings of the Lord and the Blessed Virgin are done on wood and through them God and the Blessed Virgin are honored, and they are regarded as their memorials. The servant of God is like the wood and the painting, because he is a being created by God's hand and in him God's goodness is honored. But like the painted wood, the servant of God must attribute nothing to himself, for the honor and glory are due to God alone, while shame and tribulation befit the man as long as he lives because his flesh is contrary to God's good gifts."

St. Francis wanted to be humble among his brothers. For the sake of living in greater humility, he resigned his office of governing before all the brothers at a Chapter held at St. Mary of the Portiuncula. This was a few years after his conversion. He told them, "From this moment on I am dead as far as you are concerned. See, there is Brother Peter Catanii — I and you shall all obey him!" On hearing this the brothers wept in a loud voice and shed copious tears. St. Francis knelt before Brother Peter and promised him obedience and reverence.

On arising, he joined his hands, turned his eyes up heavenwards, and said, " O Lord, I commend to you the family you gave me. Since I am disabled by illnesses and cannot bear the burden of their care, I confide them to Ministers. Wherefore, if any brother should perish because of the Ministers' neglect, or bad example, or overly harsh correction, let them be held answerable to you, O Lord, when they appear before you on the day of Judgment. "

From that moment until his death he remained a subject like any other brother.

It was his will to be subject to the Minister General and the Provincial Ministers, obeying the Minister of the Province wherever he might be staying or preaching. For the better practice of perfection and humility, he said to his Minister General, once a long time before his death, " I want you to appoint a brother from among my companions who will always be with me as your proxy. I shall obey him as I would you. For the sake of good example and the virtue of obedience, I want to have him at my side at all times in life and death. " From this time until his death he always had one of his companions as Guardian, and he obeyed him as if he were the Minister General.

In fact, he said one time to his companions, " The All-highest has granted me this grace among others, that I would obey a novice who had entered the Order this very day, and do so as earnestly as I would if he were my Guardian, and as if he were the brother who was first and of longest standing in the life and Order of the brothers. The subject should see not the man in his superior, but the One for whose love he has made himself a subject."

He also said, "Nowhere in the whole world is there a superior who would be so greatly feared by his subjects and brothers as the Lord would have me feared by my brothers if I should will it. But the All-highest himself has conferred upon me this grace that I want to be content with all that happens just like the least brother in the Order."

We who were with him have often seen with our own eyes that he conducted himself as he declared in his words. On a number of occasions when brothers failed to give proper attention to his needs, or made some remark to him that ordinarily would make a man angry, he would go right away to pray. On returning he would no longer have any mind to remember it and would not make any such comment as, "That brother didn't take care of what I needed," or "He said such and such a thing to me."

He wanted to be poor: From the time he began to have brothers until the day of his death he would refuse to have or to wear in this world anything more than one tunic — although it could be patched on the inside and the outside — a cord and breeches.

As a matter of fact, at one time during his illness, for the sake of greater perfection and poverty, he gave over all his companions to the Minister General, telling him, "I do not want to have a special companion. Rather, for the love of the Lord God, when I am in a particular place, the brothers of that place may provide for me and accompany me according to however the Lord may inspire them. " He also said, " I have seen a blind man who had only a little dog to guide him along his road. "

The closer he came to death, the more painstaking he·was in considering diligently how he could live and die in total humility and poverty.

Brother Bernard is first in St. Francis's love

Brother Bernard eats the cookies — the Saint's exceptional regard for him as first companion — Brother Bernard was long tried by demons — the Saint's prophecy of his final peace and consolation — the last days of Brother Bernard — the Passover of cherries — the smiling saint.

On the day when Lady Jacoba prepared her pastries for St. Francis, the holy Father remembered Brother Bernard and said to his companions, " Brother Bernard likes these cookies. " He called one of his companions to him and said, " Please tell Brother Bernard to come to me right away. " The brother went immediately and brought him in to St. Francis. Brother Bernard sat down by the bed where St. Francis lay and said, " Father, I ask you to bless me and show me your love. If you show your love for me with paternal affection, I believe that God himself, and all the other brothers of the Order will love me more. " St. Francis was unable to see him because he had lost his eyesight

53

many days before. He stretched out his right hand and placed it on the head of Brother Giles who was the third of the first brothers, and who at the moment was sitting beside Brother Bernard. He intended putting it on Brother Bernard's head. He felt Brother Giles' head in that way a blind man has of touching, and through the Holy Spirit knew right away what he had done. He said, " This is not the head of my Brother Bernard! " Brother Bernard quickly moved closer to him. St. Francis layed his hand on his head and blessed him.

He said moreover to one of the brothers, " Write down what I tell you. The first brother the Lord gave me was Brother Bernard, and he was the first one to undertake and fulfill in all perfection the perfection of the Holy Gospel by giving away all his goods to the poor. For this reason, and in consideration of many other prerogatives, I must have greater love for him than for any other brother in the whole Order. Wherefore I will and ordain, insofar as it is in my power, that whoever the Minister General may be, he should love him as if he were me. And may the Provincial Ministers and the brothers of the whole Order look upon him as my proxy. " Brother Bernard was greatly consoled by this as were the brothers looking on.

At one time St. Francis was considering Brother Bernard's perfection. He made a prophecy about him while some other brothers listened. He said, " I tell you that some of the most powerful and insidious demons have been assigned to Brother Bernard to try him. But toward the end of his life, the merciful Lord will withdraw from him all his tribulation and temptation, both internal and external, and give holy peace, rest and consolation to his spirit and body.

"All the brothers who will see this happen or hear about it will be overwhelmed with admiration and believe it a wondrous miracle, and he will pass from this world to the Lord in that peace, rest, and consolation of both inner and outer man."

The brothers who had heard St. Francis say these things marveled greatly because what he had, by the Holy Spirit, foretold truly took place, to the letter, and point by point.

In fact, when Brother Bernard was on his deathbed, he was blessed with such peace and tranquillity of spirit that he did not want to lie down in his bed. When he lay down he was practically sitting up. He did not want the slightest vapor of his humors to mount to his head and bring on imaginings and dream fantasies that would be something other than what pertained to thoughts about God.

If anything of the sort happened, he would quickly sit up, hit himself, and say, "What was that? Why did I think such a thing?"

He had liked to comfort himself by putting rosewater to his nose. When he came closer to death, he no longer had this done because he did not want his continuous meditation upon God to be disturbed. When anyone offered it, he would say, "Don't hinder me!" In like manner, so as to die more willingly, peacefully and tranquilly, he dispossessed himself of the right to govern his body. He put it in the charge of a brother who was a doctor and was attending him. He said, "I want to have nothing to do with saying what I eat or drink. You take charge. If you give, I take; if you don't, then no."

He requested holy unction, and when the brothers came vested and were preparing to anoint him, the vase containing the holy oil suddenly broke. Brother Peregrinus of the Marches, a spiritual and holy man, a companion of Brother Bernard at the time, remarked humorously in a low voice, "Look, the alabaster jar of ointment has been broken, and now copious graces will descend and spread all around."

While he was being anointed, Brother Bernard could no longer restrain himself. He was used to keeping his thoughts to himself. Now he broke forth in tears. He called the brothers to him, dropped to his knees on the ground, and accused himself of all his faults. He said, "I was never a Lesser Brother unless I was being tempted. The Lord came to my aid in my temptations." He asked the brothers to pray for him devoutly, "But mostly I ask you this," he said, "that when you pray on my account, you pray for yourselves too."

On Friday someone brought him a basket of·cherries. He said to the brothers with him, and to the brother who was his doctor, "Give me some cherries and let me eat some, for this is the last time I shall ever eat. I ask you to eat with me and make a Passover with me." He could not withold his tears while he ate. The brothers then began saying, "Truly he was a saint and no one knew

56

it!" The brothers wept and exulted with joy because they saw that he was a saint of the Lord.

From the time his illness began he had wanted a brother priest to be nearby at all times until the hour of death. When anything came to mind that reproached his conscience, he immediately confessed it and acknowledged his fault.

After he died, his skin turned white and his flesh became soft. His face looked as if he were smiling. After his death he looked fairer than before, and all who saw him liked looking at him then more than when he was alive because he seemed to be a smiling saint.

Lady Clare sees St. Francis the last time

St. Clare fears she will die before seeing St. Francis — his prophetic reply to her message — St. Francis's triumphant cortege — his body is brought to St. Damien's — a reference to the grating indicates that the Sisters were still at St. Damien's at the time of writing (they left in 1260 or before).

Lady Clare, the first little plant of the Order of the sisters, Abbess of the Poor Sisters of the Monastery of St. Damien of Assisi, who emulated St. Francis in persevering observance of the poverty of the Son of God, was extremely ill in the week in which St. Francis died. Fearing that she would die before St. Francis did, she wept and sorrowed, and could not be consoled because she might not see St. Francis, her one father after God, before she would die. He had been the one who had consoled her inwardly and outwardly, and it had been he who first gave her a firm foundation in the grace of God.

She had one of the brothers go to St. Francis and tell him how troubled she was. St. Francis had cherished her and her sisters with fatherly affection because of their holy mode of life. When he got her message, he felt deep pity for her, because it was just a few years after he had begun to have brothers when she had been converted to God, with the Lord's help, through his counsels. Her conversion had been a source of edification not only for the Order of the Brothers, but as well for the universal Church of God.

St. Francis realized that her longing to see him could not possibly be satisfied because both of them were gravely ill. To console her, he wrote a letter bringing her his blessing and his pardon for anything in which she had been remiss, if indeed she had ever been, in fulfilling his commands and wishes, and those of the Son of God. He also told her that she should set aside all sorrow, and let herself be consoled in the Lord. It was not he but the Spirit of God who spoke the words when he told the brother she had sent, "Go and take this letter to Lady Clare. Tell her that even though she may not see me at this moment, she should put aside all sorrow and sadness. Let her know that truly she is going to see me before her death, as her sisters will too, and they will be greatly consoled on my account."

It came about that shortly afterwards St. Francis passed away during the night. The next morning, all the people of the city of Assisi, men, women, and clergy, took the holy body, and singing hymns, all holding tree branches, bore the body from the place where he had died, as the Lord willed, to St. Damien's. Thus the word was fulfilled which the Lord had spoken in his Saint for the consolation of his daughters and handmaids.

They removed the iron grating through which the handmaids of Christ are accustomed to receive Holy Communion, and through which at times they hear the word of God preached. The brothers then took the holy body from the litter and held it in their arms at the window for a good hour, allowing Lady Clare and her Sisters to have as much consolation as they could from it. Of course, their tears overflowed and they felt crushed with grief because after God, he had been their one consolation in this world.

The larks' adieu

The wonderful visit of the larks on the eve of the Saint's death — words on St. Francis's affectionate regard for the larks — his special veneration for the Lord's Nativity — the lark is a good example for his Religious.

On Saturday evening after vespers before the night when St. Francis passed to the Lord, many birds called *praises*, which are larks, took to flying not very high over the roof of the house where he lay. They circled about in wheel formation and sang.

We who were with St. Francis and who have written these things about him have heard him say many times, "If I were to speak to the Emperor, I would implore him that for the love of God and my supplications he establish by written decree that no-one may capture our sisters the larks or harm them in any way. Likewise all mayors of cities and lords of castle towns and villages should be required to oblige the people, on the feast of the Lord's Nativity each year, to throw wheat grains and other grains along the roads outside their cities and castles, so as to provide something to eat for our sisters the larks and other birds in view of the great solemnity of the day. Also in reverence to the Son of God whom the Holy Virgin Mother placed in a manger between the ox and the ass that night, every man must give fodder in plenty on the eve of the Nativity to our brothers the oxen and the asses. Furthermore, on the feast of the Lord's Nativity, the rich must see to it that the poor are given their fill to eat."

St. Francis held the feast of the Lord's Nativity in greater reverence than any other of his solemnities. Although we find our Lord working our salvation in the other solemnities, he would say, the fact of his being born for us required that our salvation be accomplished.

Insomuch he wanted every Christian to exult in the Lord on that day, and for the love of him who gave himself to us, every man should give generously and with joy not only to the poor but also to the beasts and birds.

St. Francis had this to say about the larks: " Sister

Lark wears a hood like the Religious, and she is a humble bird. She hops gaily along the road looking for bits of grain for herself. If she finds them mixed in the beasts' dung, she just plucks them out and eats them. When she is in flight she praises the Lord like a good Religious who despises earthly things and whose thoughts are ever set upon heavenly things. Furthermore, her clothing, that is her feathers, is earth color and in this she gives the Religious good example. They should not wear clothing that is colorful and made of fine cloth, but rather it should be as if dead, earth-like. "

Since St. Francis found the above-mentioned things in our sisters the larks, he loved them affectionately and it delighted him to see them.

Demons in the Lord's service

St. Francis wants solitude in the city of Rome — he is assailed by demons — he explains that the demons are the Lord's sheriffs — the benefit of chastisement — St. Francis must give moral support to the brothers by enduring hardships.

At one time, St. Francis went to Rome to visit the Lord Hugolin, Bishop of Ostia, who later became pope, and was his guest there for a while. After taking leave of him, he visited the Lord Leo, Cardinal of the Holy Cross. This Cardinal was a very kind and gracious man, and was glad to see St. Francis whom he held in reverence and esteem. He invited him most devoutly to be his guest for a while since it was wintertime and very cold. The weather was stormy and there was wind and rain almost every day as was usual at the season. He told St. Francis, "Brother, this is hardly the time for journeying on foot. I should like, if it is your pleasure, to have you stay with me until the weather is more suitable for foot travel. It is my custom to provide meals for a certain number of poor men in my house every day. I would have food served you just as if you were one of those paupers."

The Lord Cardinal spoke in this way because he well knew that St. Francis in his humility always wanted to be treated like any pauper wherever he was received as a guest, even though his sanctity was so outstanding that he was revered as a saint by the Lord Pope, the Cardinals, and all the grand secular personages who knew him.

He added, "I shall place at your disposition a house that will serve your purposes well in a secluded spot where you can pray and take your meals, if that would suit you." Brother Angelus de Tancredi, one of the first twelve brothers, was staying with the Lord Cardinal at the time. He said to St. Francis, "Brother, near here, in the wall of Rome, there is a fine tower. It is large and roomy inside, and there are nine vaulted chambers. You could use them, and be as secluded there as you would be in a hermitage." St. Francis answered, "Let's go and see it." When he saw it, he liked it. He came back to the Cardinal and said, "Lord, perhaps I will stay with you a while." The Cardinal was very glad to hear this.

Brother Angelus then went and got the place ready so that St. Francis could stay there with his companion both day and night. St. Francis did not want to go out either at night or during the day while staying with the Lord Cardinal. Brother Angelus offered to bring meals for St. Francis and his companion every day. He would leave the food outside the door because neither he nor anyone else was to go in to him. St. Francis and his companion thereupon went to dwell there.

On the first night after he had gone to bed, demons came and gave him a terrible beating. He immediately called his companion who was staying a good distance away from him. He cried, " Come here! " and the brother rushed to him. St. Francis told him, " Brother, demons have given me a terrible beating. I want you to stay close by me. I am afraid to stay here alone. " The companion stayed at his side the whole night. St. Francis was trembling all over like a man with fever. Both stayed awake the whole night.

During the night St. Francis talked with his companion. He said to him, " Why is it that the demons beat me, and why does the Lord let them have the power to harm me ? " He went on to say, " Those demons are the Lord's sheriffs. The mayor of a town sends a sheriff to punish a man if he has committed an offense. In the same way, the Lord corrects and chastises those whom he loves through the agency of his sheriffs, who in this case are demons. Actually, they are ministers in his service.

" It often happens that a perfect Religious will sin and be unaware of his sin. Even if he does not know what

63

his sin is, the devil will punish him. The Religious will then set about examining himself carefully, and scrutinizing his inner and outer acts, until he finds out what his offense has been because the Lord leaves nothing unpunished during the earthly life of those whom he tenderly loves.

"As for myself, thanks to God's mercy and grace, there is no offence I know of which I have not atoned through confession and acts of reparation. In his mercy, the Lord has given me the grace to know, when in prayer, what it is I can do that will please him, and also what would displease him.

"In this case, it seems to me that the Lord could have had his sheriffs punish me for this reason: Although the Cardinal was quite pleased to treat me kindly, and my body did need the attention, and I could accept his kindness with an easy mind, I had failed to remember my duty to my brothers. They go about the world enduring hunger and severe hardships, and some live in wretched little houses and hermitages. When they hear that I am staying with the Lord Cardinal, they will have occasion to complain. They could say, 'We put up with such and such hardships, and he has his comforts!' I am bound at all times to set a good example, because I was given to them for this purpose. The brothers will be the better edified if I stay with them in their wretched little places, and share their lives with them, than if I stay elsewhere. They will bear their hardships with greater patience when they are told and may know that I bear the same trials they do."

It is true that St. Francis was always ailing, for he

had been weak and feeble by nature while he was living in the world, and he became daily feebler because of illnesses until the day of his death. He believed nevertheless that he was obliged to give good example to the brothers and reject whatever could give them cause for complaint. He wanted to allow no pretext for the brothers to say, "He has his needs taken care of, but we don't!" Whether he was in good or bad health, until he died, he willed to suffer drastic hardships. If any of the brothers knew what we know who were with him for a considerable time and remained with him until the day of his death, and if they would recall to memory what he had endured, they would not be able to hold back their tears. Then when they would have to undergo any hardships and tribulations, they would bear them with greater patience.

St. Francis left the tower as soon as morning dawned, and went to the Lord Cardinal. He told him everything that had happened to him during the night, and what he had already told his companion. He remarked as well, "Men have great faith in me, and believe me a holy man. Now see, the demons have thrown me out of my hermit's cell!" He had wanted to stay in seclusion for prayer as if in a hermit's cell and talk with nobody but his companion.

The Lord Cardinal was well pleased with him. He knew and revered him as a saint, and was insomuch satisfied with St. Francis's decision to stay there no longer. So, St. Francis took leave of him and journeyed to the hermitage of St. Francis at Fonte Colombo near Rieti.

Both graces and torments on Mount Alverna

St. Francis invokes a sign of the Lord's will — his
contemplation must not be a pretext for avoiding the
labors of preaching — birds give the sign — he received
not only graces including the visit of the Seraph but
also demoniacal torments.

At one time St. Francis went to the hermitage on
Mount Alverna. He liked that place because it
was far away from everything and secluded. He
had chosen it as the place for a forty-day retreat in honor
of St. Michael, and arrived there before the feast of the
Assumption of the glorious Virgin Mary. Counting the
days from the feast of St. Mary to the feast of St. Michael,
he would spend forty days there in all. He said, "In
honor of God and the Blessed Virgin Mary, his Mother,
and St. Michael, prince of angels and souls, I want to
make my forty-day retreat here."

He went into the cell where he expected to remain
continuously for prayer, and on the first night prayed the
Lord to show him by some sign he could recognize
whether it was his will that he remain there. St. Francis
was always careful to ascertain whether it was the Lord's
will that he stay some place in continuous prayer or
whether he should travel about in the world to preach.

He feared lest at times, under the semblance of a desire
to remain in seclusion for prayer, it was really the body
wanting its ease, and was refusing the labor entailed in
going about in the world to preach, which was what

Christ had come down from heaven to do. In fact, he would ask the persons he thought were beloved of the Lord to pray and ask him to make known to them what his will was, whether it be for him to go about in the world preaching, or whether it be keeping to his seclusion and prayer.

When the following morning dawned and he was in prayer, birds of many different kinds flew over the cell where he stayed. They did not come in a flock all at one time, but first one would come and sing, making its song ever so sweet, and then fly away again. Then another would come, sing, and fly away, and so did they all. St. Francis was filled with wonder and was delightfully consoled. He pondered then upon what the meaning of this could be. He became aware that the Lord was speaking to him within his spirit and telling him, "This is a sign that the Lord is going to do good things for you in this cell, and he will give you many consoling graces."

This truly came to pass, because along with the many other graces, both hidden and manifest, that were bestowed upon him there, was the vision of the Seraph shown him by the Lord which was to remain a wonderful consolation between him and his Lord in his soul for the rest of his life. When his companion brought him his meal that day, St. Francis told him what had happened.

Even though he was to have great consolations in that cell, the demons tormented him cruelly at nighttime, as he told his companion. On one occasion he said, "If the brothers were to know how terribly the demons torment me, there is not a one of them who would not pity me and feel compassion for me." It was for this reason, as he often explained to his companions, that he could not give the brothers more satisfactory attention or grant the more frequent companionship they desired of him.

The devil slyly hides in a pillow

The saint is persuaded to use a pillow — he is cruelly tormented — his companion is held motionless — the devil's tactics are described.

At one time St. Francis was staying at the hermitage of Greccio. He stayed to pray in the last cell, located behind the main one, and would not leave it by day or by night. One night, shortly after he had gone to bed, he called his companion who slept in the main cell, the old one, and was not far away from him. The companion got up right away and came to him. He entered the yard and stood at the door of the cell where St. Francis lay. The holy Father told him, "Brother, tonight I could neither sleep nor stay up and pray. My head is swimming and my bones are still a-tremble. I feel as if I had eaten bread made from tares." His companion then talked over these things with him and gave him sympathy.

St. Francis said, "I believe the devil was hiding inside that pillow I have under my head." Lord John of Greccio had got a feather pillow for him the day before. He was a man that the Saint loved affectionately and whom he regarded as a friend throughout his lifetime.

After St. Francis had left the world, he would not sleep on a mattress nor have a feather pillow under his head when he was ill or at any other time. In view of his condition, ill and suffering from his eye disease, the brothers had brought such force of persuasion to bear upon him that he gave way to them and took the pillow even though he did not want it.

He tossed the pillow to his companion who put out his right arm, caught it, placed it on his left shoulder and held it there with his right hand. He then walked out of the yard.

Of a sudden he lost his speech, and was unable to leave the spot where he stood. He could move neither his arm nor his hand, nor could he drop the pillow. He simply stood there. He had the sensation of a man taken leave of himself, who was neither aware of himself or of anything else. He stood that way for more than an hour when by divine mercy St. Francis called him. Immediately he came back to himself and threw the pillow behind him. He returned to St. Francis and told him what had happened. St. Francis then said to him, " In the evening while I was reciting Compline, I knew it when the devil came in the cell. " Later he knew for certain it was the devil keeping him from sleep and not letting him stay up and pray either.

He explained to his companion, " The devil is sly and clever. Thanks to God's mercy and grace he hasn't the power to harm my soul. To attack me, he hampers the doings of my body. He keeps me from sleeping and then won't let me stay up to pray either. This is his way of hindering my devotion and stifling the joy of my heart, and getting me to complain about my ailments."

For many years he suffered ailments of the stomach, spleen and liver, and he had an eye disease. And yet, he was so devout and prayed so reverently that at the time of prayer he would not lean against the wall or a partition, but always stand up straight, and without using his hood to cover his head. He would though sometimes kneel. This was his custom even when spending the greater part of the day and the night in prayer.

When he traveled about the country on foot he would always make a halt when the time came to recite his Hours. If he were riding, and this could happen because he was always weak with illness, he would dismount to say his Hours. For instance, at one time he was returning from Rome where he had been briefly the guest of the Lord Leo. It rained the whole day. Being extremely ill at the time, he was riding horseback. He got down from his horse and stood at the roadside to say his Hours, even though the rain was pouring down and he was soaked through.

He would say, "The body wants to eat its meals in peace and quiet, and both the meals and the body become food for the worms. How much peace and quiet should the soul have then when the food it eats is God himself!"

He would also say, "How happy it makes the devil when he succeeds in hindering or stifling the spirit of prayer and the joy of heart that flow from purified prayer and other good works of a servant of God! When the devil manages to get something of his own lodged in a servant of God, that servant of God, if he be wise, will get rid of it as quickly as he can by contrition, confession, and the works of reparation. If he fails to do this, the devil will lose no time in making a big log out of a hair, for he keeps on adding to what he has put there. "

He would also say, " The servant of God must be prudent and make provision for the body's needs' in matters of eating, sleeping and other necessities. He should not let Brother Body have grounds to complain and say, 'I can't keep standing on my feet for long prayer sessions, or be joyful in hardships and do other good works for a man who doesn't take care of my needs'.'"

Likewise he said that if the servant of God is prudent and gives care that is good enough and suitable to his bodily needs, within the measure of his possibilities, and still Brother Body insists upon being lazy, negligent, and sleepy-headed in prayer and vigils and other good works of the soul, then he must chastise it just as he would a stubborn and lazy beast. It is willing enough to eat, but it has no will to render service or bear its burden. But if it is because of want and poverty that Brother Body's needs in sickness and health cannot be taken care of, and if the necessities have been requested of a brother or superior for the love of God and they are not granted, then the servant of God should endure his hardship. The Lord will attribute it to him as martyrdom. He did what it was his part to do when he requested what he needed; he is excused, and commits no sin even though his body becomes the weaker for it.

St. Francis dealt harshly and severely with his body from the beginning of his conversion until the day of his death, but his chief and most particular concern was seeing to it that inwardly and outwardly he would be and remain spiritually joyful. He said that if the servant of God would always strive to have and keep inner and outer joy, the fruit of a pure heart, the demons would have no power to harm him. They would say, " This servant of God is joyful in tribulation and joyful when all goes well. We can't find an entrance to get in and do him damage. "

On one occasion he reproved a companion because it seemed to him he was sad and had a sorrowful expression on his face. He asked him, " Why are you sad and sorrowful for your sins ? Let the matter be kept between you and God. Pray to him and ask him in his mercy to restore the joy of his salvation to your soul. Then see if you can't be cheerful when you are with me or the others. It is not fitting that a servant of God let himself be seen by his brother or anyone else downcast and with a woeful look on his face. "

He also said, " I know that the demons envy me when they see what good gifts the Lord in his mercy has granted me. Since they cannot get at me to harm me in my own soul, they contrive to harm me through my companions. But if they find they can't harm either me or my companions, then they will be routed and take to flight. Thus if ever I'm being tried by temptations and in a bad humor,

I can look at my companion, see how he is filled with joy, and because of his cheerfulness leave the temptation and bad humor behind and get back my inner joy. "

Spiritual training of the early Brothers

Compassionate treatment of a hungry brother — teaching of prudence in ascetical practices — poverty must prevail — the brothers should beg cheerfully to imitate the Lord's poverty — literal application of gospel teachings.

Once at the time when the Order was just beginning, that is, when St. Francis had just begun to have some brothers, he was dwelling with them at Rivotorto. One night, about midnight, when everybody was in bed sleeping, a brother cried out, "I'm dying! I'm dying!" The brothers were startled and terrified, and they all woke up. St. Francis got up and said, "Get up, brothers, and light the light!"

When the light was lit, St. Francis said, "Who said 'I'm dying'?" The brother answered, "I did." St. Francis asked him, "What's the matter, brother? What are you dying of?" He replied, "I'm dying of hunger."

St. Francis was a man who was all charity and consideration. So that the brother would not be ashamed eating alone, he had the table set, and had everybody get up and eat with him. This brother and some others had

73

been newly converted to the Lord, and were mortifying their bodies to the extreme.

When they had finished eating, St. Francis said to the brothers, "My brothers, I must tell you that each of you should take into consideration his own nature. Perhaps one of you can get along with less food than another, but I don't want any of you who needs more food to try to imitate someone who can do with less. Each should take stock of his own nature, and provide his body with what it needs. Just as we must be careful to avoid overeating, for this would be bad for both body and soul, so must we be careful about excessive fasting, and particularly because the Lord wills mercy and not sacrifice (*Mt* 9,13)."

He went on to say, "My dear brothers, for the sake of charity I have had us all eat together so that a single brother would not feel ashamed having to eat alone. I had to do this because both necessity and charity called for it. Nevertheless, I tell you, I don't want to do it again. It wouldn't be behavior for Religious, nor would it be virtuous. Rather, it is my will and command that each of you satisfy your body's needs insofar as our state of poverty permits."

The first brothers, and those who followed them for a long time, mortified their bodies extremely, not only by abstaining from food and drink, but also by vigils, by putting up with the cold, and by manual labor. Those who could get them wore iron bands and hauberks against the flesh underneath their tunics. Others wore the heaviest hairshirts they could get.

The holy Father found that such practices could make the brothers ill, and that in fact some had recently become ill.

At a certain Chapter he forbade the brothers to wear anything against the flesh excepting the tunic.

We who were with him testify that from the time he began to have brothers with him, and throughout his lifetime, he was prudent, although taking care that they did not deviate at any time from the way of poverty proper to our Order in matters of food and the articles they used. In this he followed the norms of the very early brothers.

He himself, from the time he was converted, before he had any brothers, and throughout his lifetime, dealt severely with his own body, even though by nature he had been frail and weak as a boy, and while he was in the world he had had to be fastiduously attentive to the way he lived.

There came a time when he noticed that the brothers had begun to go beyond the limits of poverty and virtue in their food and the articles they used. Thereupon he preached a sermon and spoke to the brothers there present as to representatives of all the brothers. He said, " Do my brothers suppose that food is not necessary for my body too ? Yet since I am called upon to be the model and example for all the brothers, I will be contented with very little food and use articles that are not fine. "

When St. Francis began to have brothers he was extremely happy about their conversion, and rejoiced because the Lord had granted him good companions. He loved and respected them so much that he would not tell them to go out and beg for alms. He thought they would be ashamed to go begging. He preferred to spare them embarrassment going out by himself to beg for alms every day. However this was too exhausting for his body, for he had been delicate and frail by nature in the world, and he was now still weaker after practicing rigid fasting and mortification from the day he had left the world.

Finding he could not stand the exertion, he took into consideration that the others had also been called to beg alms, whether they felt ashamed or not, and that they did not yet realize clearly that it was their duty, nor did they have the courage of their convictions to say, "We want to go begging for alms." So he said to them, "My dear brothers and sons, you must not be ashamed to go begging for alms, since the Lord made himself poor for our sakes in this world. It is because of his example that we have chosen the way of truest poverty, and it was the way of his holy Mother. Such is the heritage our Lord Jesus Christ gained for us and left to us and to all who want to live according to his example of holy poverty."

He also said, "I tell you truly that many men will come from the highest nobility and from among the most learned scholars of the world to our community, and will esteem it a high honor to beg alms with the blessing of the Lord God. You should go out more willingly and with a more joyful spirit than the man who goes offering a hundred pieces of silver for a penny because what you have to offer is the love of God to those from whom you

76

beg the alms telling them, 'Give us alms for the love of the Lord God!' Indeed, compared with God's love earth and heaven are as nothing."

They were still too few to be sent out two by two. He sent them singly to the castle towns and villages. When they came back, each showed St. Francis the alms he had collected, and they would say one to another, "I got more alms than you did." St. Francis was happy to see them so gay and cheerful. From that time on each of them was glad to ask permission to go out and beg for alms.

At that same time, when St. Francis was with the brothers he then had, his purity was such that from the hour in which the Lord revealed to him that they should live, both he and his brothers, according to the norms of the Holy Gospel, he wanted to practice it to the letter, and he strove to do so the whole of his lifetime. He therefore forbade the brother who did the cooking to prepare for the next day's meals by putting the vegetables in hot water the evening before, as was customary. They should rather observe the Holy Gospel where it is said, "Do not be solicitous for the morrow (*Mt* 6,34)." So the brother would put them to soak after Matins had been said.

For a long time his words were followed by many brothers, and in a number of places where they lived independently, especially in the cities where they would not collect or accept more alms at one time than were enough for one day.

Thoughtful regard for a sick Brother

In early years the brothers spurned bodily needs —
St. Francis treats a sick brother compassionately.

One time, while St. Francis was at the same place, a brother was staying there who was a very spiritual man and had been in the Order from the early days. He was at the time extremely weak and ailing. Seeing him in this condition, St. Francis was moved by compassion for him.

At that time, whether the brothers were in good or bad health, they cheerfully and patiently practiced poverty as their abundance. They would even do without medicines when they were ill. Rather they preferred what was contrary to the body's needs.

In the case of this brother, St. Francis said to himself, "If that brother should eat ripe grapes in the early morning, I think it would do him good." One day. he got up secretly in the early morning, called that brother, and took him into the vineyard next to the church. He found a vine on which the grapes were sound and good for eating. He sat down by the vine with the brother beside him and began to eat grapes. Thus he thoughtfully avoided embarrassing the brother by not having him eat the grapes alone. While they ate, the brother praised the Lord God, and as long as he lived he would frequently tell the other brothers, devoutly and shedding tears, what mercy the holy Father had shown him.

St. Francis in prayer

The bishop is ejected as by an invisible force from the Saint's presence.

At one time when St. Francis was at the same place, he would go to pray in a cell which was located at the back of the house. The bishop of Assisi came to see him one day while he was there. He came to the house, knocked on the door so as to go in to St. Francis, and opening the door for himself, walked into the cell within which was the little cell made of matting where St. Francis was. Knowing that the holy Father considered him a close friend and loved him, he went ahead and lifted the matting of the little cell expecting to go in and see him. He had no sooner put his head into the little cell than suddenly, willy-nilly, he was shoved back forcefully by the will of the Lord, for he was not worthy of looking upon him. He withdrew walking backwards. As quickly as he could he got out of the cell trembling and amazed. He confessed his fault before all the brothers, and declared that he was very sorry he had come that day.

Compassionate help to a tempted brother

A brother· is tormented by temptations — St. Francis perceives his hidden trouble — he advises that confession is not required for temptations — through his merits the brother's peace is restored.

There was a certain brother, a spiritual man, who had been in the Order for a long time, and was an intimate companion of St. Francis. There was a period when he passed many days tempted grievously and cruelly from suggestions of the devil. So severely was he tried that he was practically reduced to the depths of despair. Each day he was plagued by these torments and was ashamed to confess so often. For this reason he was mortifying himself severely by abstinence, vigils, shedding tears, and scourgings. He had been enduring these daily torments for many days when St. Francis, by divine dispensation, came to the place.

One day St. Francis was walking with two of the brothers, including the one who was being tormented. St. Francis drew away a piece from the one brother, and joined the one who was in tribulation. He said to him, "Dear brother, it is my will, and I am telling you, that henceforth you are not held to confess those suggestions and inspirations of the devil to anyone. Do not fear; they have not harmed your soul. I give you permission to say seven *Our Father's* whenever you are tormented by those suggestions."

The brother was made very happy by St. Francis

telling him he was not bound to confess those things, for having to make a daily confession of them threw him into great confusion, and was the chief cause of his distress. The brother marveled at the holy Father's sanctity, for he had known of the temptations only through the Holy Spirit. This was evident because he had confessed to no one but the priests. Indeed he had gone to a number of different priests in his embarrassment, for he would have been ashamed to let any one priest know about the whole of his weakness and temptation.

From that very hour he was freed inwardly and outwardly from the great tribulation he had been enduring for such a long time, and by the grace of God he was granted tranquillity and peace of soul and body through the merits of St. Francis.

The need of a church

St. Francis discusses the need of a church with his brothers — it should be small and poor — it is needed for recitation of divine office along with space for dwellings and cemetery.

When St. Francis saw that it was the Lord's will to multiply the number of the brothers, he said to them, "My dear brothers and sons, I see that the Lord wills that we grow and become more numerous. Therefore it seems to me a good thing, and befitting the religious life that we obtain from the bishop, or the canons of St. Rufinus, or from the abbot of the Monastery

of St. Benedict a small and poor little church where the brothers could recite their Hours. There should be nothing more attached to it than a small and poor house built from mud and wickerwork where the brothers could sleep and take care of their needs. The place we have now is not proper, and this house is too small for the brothers to live in since it is the Lord's pleasure that our numbers increase. Moreover, we have no church where the brothers can recite their Hours, and if anyone should die, this would not be a worthy place for his burial, nor should he be buried in a church of the diocesan priests."
What St. Francis said was agreeable to the other brothers.

The Benedictines grant St. Mary of the Angels to the brothers

A request is made first of the bishop, then of the cathedral canons, and last of the Benedictines — the abbot grants the Portiuncula with the condition that it be the center of the Order.

Thereupon St. Francis went to see the bishop of Assisi and made the proposal he had discussed with the brothers. The bishop replied, "Brother, I have no such church to give you." He went to the canons of St. Rufinus and made the same proposal and they gave the same reply. Then he went to the monastery of St. Benedict on Mount Subasio, and made the same proposal to the abbot as he had made to the bishop and the canons, informing him of the reply the others had given him.

The abbot, in his piety, felt he should do something about it and discussed the proposal with his brothers. The Lord willing it, they granted St. Francis and his brothers the church of St. Mary of the Portiuncula as the poorest church they had. It was the poorest little church in the countryside round about the city of Assisi, and this was what St. Francis had long been desiring.

The abbot told him, "Brother, we have granted your request. However, it is our desire that if the Lord should increase your community this place would be the head of all the brothers of your Order." This condition was agreeable to St. Francis and the other brothers.

Some information on St. Mary of the Angels

St. Francis is pleased because of the dedication to St. Mary, and because of the church's poverty and small size — it is to become the mother and head of the Order — the reason for the name Portiuncula — it is in bad condition but retains the affections of the people — the Order grows swiftly after being established here — the original dedication to St. Mary of the Angels — neither this place nor any other to be held in ownership — it is especially loved by the Virgin Mary — to be held in reverence by the brothers.

St. Francis was overjoyed with the place granted to the brothers because the church bore the name of the Mother of God, because it was such a very poor little church, and because the name *Portiuncula* was associated with it. Because of this name it prefigured that it was to become the mother and head of the poor Lesser Brothers.

It was called *Portiuncula* (a small portion with respect to a patrimony) because that name had been given to the piece of land on which it was built in ancient times. St. Francis said, "The Lord willed that no other church be granted to the first brothers, and that they should build no other because this one is prophetic. The prophecy was fulfilled with the coming of the Lesser Brothers."

Although the church was a very little one and in such bad repair that it was almost in ruins, the people of the city of Assisi and the surrounding country had never ceased holding it in pious affection, and at the present day their devotion for it has grown. Thus as soon as the brothers went there to live, the Lord increased their numbers almost daily, and their fame spread throughout the whole valley of Spoleto.

In ancient times the church was called St. Mary of the Angels but the people of the neighboring countryside called it St. Mary of the Portiuncula. After the brothers had begun to restore it, the men and women of the region would say, "Let's go to St. Mary of the Angels."

The abbot and the monks had given the church freely to St. Francis and his brothers without demanding anything by way of tribute or annual rent. Nevertheless, St. Francis as a good and wise master who builds upon firm rock — that is to say, he founded his community upon extreme poverty — would send a basket of little fishes, called whitebate, once a year to the abbot. He did this as a sign of more perfect humility and poverty intending that the brothers would have no place as their own property, nor live in any place which was not subject to someone else's ownership, and thus have no power of selling or alienating property in any way whatsoever.

When the brothers brought their yearly offering of little fishes, the monks would give St. Francis and the brothers a jar of oil in acknowledgment of St. Francis's humility, since he had made the offering of his own free will.

We who were with St. Francis testify that he made certain declarations about that church. He said that because of the great privilege the Lord had manifested and revealed to him in that place, he was assured that among all the churches of this world which the Blessed Virgin loves, she loved this one most. Insomuch he held it in the greatest reverence and devotion during the whole of his lifetime. Also, so that the brothers would always have a memorial in their hearts, he had it written in his *Testament* about the time of his death, that the brothers should do likewise. About the time of his death he declared before the Minister General and other brothers, "I want to dispose and leave in testament to the brothers that the place of St. Mary of the Portiuncula be always held in the greatest reverence and devotion."

Exemplary life at St. Mary of the Angels

Norms for silence and conversation — ascetical practices — work as discipline with recompense in alms for the love of God — the Minister General's responsibility for preventing laxity — idle talk and news of worldly affairs forbidden — a model community for protection of other brothers and Poor Clares.

S t. Francis continued saying: "Our brothers did so in the early days. Although it was a holy place, they duly fostered its holiness with continuous prayer, day and night, and with continuous silence. If anyone should speak after the established time for silence, it would be to speak devoutly and virtuously of things having to do with the praise of God and the salvation of souls. If it should happen, as was rarely the case, that anyone should talk about useless or idle things, he would immediately be corrected by another brother.

"They mortified the flesh, not only by fasting, but also by many vigils, by enduring the cold and scanty clothing, and by working with their hands. So as not to remain idle, they would often go and help poor men working in their fields who would at times give them bread after the work for the love of God. They sanctified themselves and the place by these and other virtuous acts.

"Others coming after them did likewise, although to a lesser degree, for a long time. Later a greater number of brothers and other persons than formerly used to come began to gather in that place. All the brothers of the

Order needed to come there, as did anybody intending to enter the Order. Moreover, the brothers' zeal for prayer and other good works was cooled, and they became more lax than they used to be in talking about idle and useless things, and about the news of the world. For these reasons, both the brothers living there and the other Religious no longer had as much reverence and devotion for the place as was befitting and as I should wish.

"Therefore, it is my will that it always be under the authority of the Minister General, so that it will be looked after with the greatest care and solicitude. To this end, he should take pains to assign a good and holy family to the place.

"Clerics should be chosen from among the brothers of the whole Order. Those are to be selected who are the holiest and most virtuous and who are the most accomplished in reciting the divine office so that not only other people, but also the brothers themselves may listen to it gladly and with great devotion.

"For their service, prudent and virtuous men should be chosen among the brothers and holy laymen. It is also my will that no brother nor any other person excepting the Minister General and the brothers doing the serving should enter where the clerics live, and these clerics should talk with no one excepting the brothers serving them and the Minister General on his visits. It is likewise my will that the lay brothers serving them be held to abstain from telling them anything not useful for the soul, especially news of the world that has come to their ears.

"Wherefore I do not want anyone going into that place, for I want its purity and sanctity well safeguarded. Idle and useless talk is to be excluded. Rather all is to be maintained pure and holy in the singing of hymns and the praises of the Lord.

"When any of these brothers passes away, the Minister General will have another holy brother come from wherever he may be living to take the place of the one who died.

"Because it could come to pass that elsewhere the brothers, and the place where they live might fall away at some time from due purity and virtue, I want this place to remain as a mirror and model for the good of the whole Order. It should stand as a lamp burning before the throne of God and before the Blessed Virgin. Because of it the Lord may be propitiated for the failings and the faults of the brothers who are remiss, and so ever preserve and protect the Order and its little plant."

St. Francis's mind on cells and houses

St. Francis intends to destroy a house built by the Assisans for visiting brothers at the Chapter — hardships caused by inadequate lodgings — good example is more important than proper lodgings — a cell that is too fine — no cell could be called St. Francis's cell.

In those times a Chapter was held yearly at St. Mary of the Portiuncula. On the occasion of one of these Chapters that was about to be held, the people of Assisi considered the matter, taking into account that the brothers, by the grace of God had now become numerous, and every day were becoming more so, and that they could not be accommodated when they would all be convened. They would have nothing but the wretched little huts roofed with straw, and with walls made of wicker and mud, quite the same sort the brothers had made when they had first come there to live.

After making a decision in general council, the Assisans built a big house of stone and lime plaster. The work was done in a very short time, working swiftly and with ardor. However it was done without the consent of St. Francis, for he was away at the time.

When St. Francis came back from the country where he had been to attend the Chapter, he was surprised to see the house that had been built. He foresaw that when the brothers would come and see that house they would take to building, or having built, large houses in the places where they lived, and where they would be living in the future, whereas it was his will that this place should stand as norm and example for all the brothers' places.

Thus one day before the Chapter closed, he climbed onto the roof and called some brothers to come up and help him. They began to throw the tiles of the roofing to the ground, with the intention of destroying the whole house.

There were some soldiers and townsmen of Assisi standing guard on behalf of the city. Since large crowds of people, made up of laymen and foreigners, had gathered outside the place to see the brothers' Chapter, these guards were necessary for the brothers' protection.

When they saw that St. Francis and his brothers were destroying the house, they immediately came forth and called out to St. Francis, "Brother, this house belongs to the community of Assisi. We tell you that you have no right to destroy our house." St. Francis replied, "Very well, since this is your house, I will not touch it." He came down from the roof right away, and the other brothers with him. Consequently, the people of the city of Assisi for a long time held the mayor in office responsible for repairing the roof or the house if there were need for it.

At another time, the Minister General decided to build a little house that the brothers could use for sleeping and saying their Hours. It would be useful because in those days all the brothers of the Order as well as anyone intending to enter the Order came there. Almost daily the brothers would have to tire themselves out doing the work necessary for looking after such a great number of men. There was no place they could go to rest or say their Hours because they had to turn their own sleeping quarters over to the many visitors.

It was a trying situation for them, having no way to take care of their bodily needs after so much strenuous labor, and there was no secluded place they could go to for the good of their souls.

St. Francis returned to that place when the house was almost built and went to one of the cells where he slept that night. In the morning he heard the noise and commotion made by the brothers at work. He wondered what the meaning of it could be and asked a companion,

"What is all this turmoil ? What are the brothers doing ?" The companion explained the situation. Instantly St. Francis had the Minister called to him. He said, "Brother, this place is the model and example for the entire Order. I by far prefer that the brothers of the place put up with their hardships and privations for the love of God, so that the other brothers of the Order coming here will take away a good example when they return to their own places. The good example is more important than providing for the needs and the convenience of the local brothers. If instead they make provisions for their needs, then the other brothers of the Order will find an example here for putting up buildings in their own places. They will say, 'In the place of St. Mary of the Portiuncula, the first and foremost place of the brothers, they build such and such large buildings. That means we can go ahead and build proper houses in our own places instead of the kind we have which aren't fit places to live in.'"

There was a brother, a very spiritual man and very close to St. Francis who lived in a certain hermitage. It occurred to him that if St. Francis should ever come there, there would be no suitable place for his lodging. He proceeded then to build a cell for the holy Father's use in a secluded spot near the brothers' place.

Not long afterwards St. Francis came there. When that brother took him to see the cell, St. Francis said, "This cell looks quite fine to me. But if you want me to stay any length of time here, you will have to have the walls covered inside and out with rocks and tree branches."

91

The cell had not been built in masonry but in wood, and the wood had been smoothed with an axe and a blade. For St. Francis it was too fine, and the brother had the changes made as the holy Father had indicated. Indeed, the poorer and the ruder the houses of the brothers, the better he liked them, and the more willingly he stayed in them as a guest.

Once after St. Francis had spent some days praying in that cell he went outside and stood near the brothers' place. A brother joined him there. St. Francis said, "Where are you coming from, brother?" He answered, "I am coming from your cell." St. Francis replied, "You have said that it is mine. Now someone else will have to stay there; I won't."

We who were with him often heard him repeat the lines of the Gospel where it is said, "The foxes have lairs, the birds in the sky have nests, but the Son of Man has nowhere to lay his head (*Mt* 8,20)." He would also say, "When the Lord withdrew into solitude where he prayed and fasted forty days and forty nights he did not have a cell or any house made for him, but stayed in the shelter of a mountain rock." Following this example, he wanted to have neither house nor cell in this world, nor did he ever have any built for him. If by chance he should happen to say to the brothers, "Fix up this cell in such and such a way," he would thereafter refuse to stay in it because of the Gospel saying, "Do not be concerned about your needs (cf. *Lk* 12,22)."

About the time of his death he had it written in his *Testament* that all the brothers' cells and houses should be built of nothing else than mud and timbers for the better observance of poverty and humility.

Directions on the erection of friaries

The land must not exceed needs — should not be owned — the brothers are pilgrims on earth — communities should be small — the bishop's consent required — for a good apostolate the secular clergy should not be antagonized — the humble brothers should serve and respect the clergy — poverty requires a ditch and a hedge instead of a stone wall — houses and churches should be poor and small — churches of others should be used for preaching to large assemblies — better housing should not be sought lest scandal be aroused.

At one time St. Francis had gone to Siena to have his diseased eyes treated, and there stayed in the cell where after his death an oratory was built in his honor. The Lord Bonaventure questioned him while he was there. This was the man who had donated the land where the brothers had built a place. He asked, "What do you think of this place?" St. Francis replied, "Would you like me to tell you how places for the brothers should be built?" Lord Bonaventure answered, "Father, I do."

St. Francis told him, "When the brothers go into a city where they don't have a place, and find somebody who wants to give them enough land for housing, a garden, and whatever else they will need, they should first of all reckon how large the piece of land should be to satisfy their needs. Of course, they should be keeping in mind the holy poverty we have vowed, and the good example we are obliged to give in all things. "

The holy Father said this because he did not want the brothers to go beyond the bounds of poverty in providing for their houses, churches, gardens, or articles used, nor did he want them to hold any of their places by right of ownership, for they should always live in the houses they had like pilgrims and strangers. Therefore, in St. Francis's mind, the communities of the brothers should never be large. It seemed to him unlikely that they could observe the norms of strict poverty if the community were large. Such was his will from the beginning of his conversion, as it was at the end when he died, so that holy poverty would be fully observed.

St. Francis went on to say, " They should afterwards go to the bishop of the city and say, 'Lord, such and such a man, for the love of the Lord God, and for the salvation of his soul, wants to give us a piece of land of a certain size, where we can build a place. We come first to you, for you are the father and the lord of souls of the whole flock confided to your care, as you are of ours and of the other brothers who would be dwelling in that place. Therefore, we want to build there with the blessing of the Lord God and yours. "

The Saint said this because the brothers wanted to obtain spiritual profit for the people with their labors, and this would be the better accomplished if they would carry out their work at peace with the prelates and priests, and thus gain profit for both them and the people, than if they should antagonize the prelates and priests, even if they did gain the spiritual profit of the people.

He also said, "The Lord has called us to serve the faith by aiding the prelates and priests of Holy Mother Church. We are then bound at all times to love, honor and revere them as much as we possibly can. Our brothers are called Lesser Brothers because they should be humble in both name and deed with respect to other people of this world, and because at the beginning of my conversion, when I separated myself from the world and my father according to the flesh, the Lord placed his word in the mouth of the bishop of Assisi so that he could counsel me well on the service of Christ and fortify my spirit. For this reason and for the many other merits I recognize in prelates, I want to love and revere not only bishops, but poor, simple priests as well, and regard them all as my masters.

"After receiving the bishop's blessing, they should have a large ditch dug all around the piece of land, and have a thick hedge planted by way of wall as a sign of their poverty and humility. When this has been done, they should have small, poor houses made from mud and timbers, and erect some cells where the brothers can go for prayer or work.

"Having individual cells favors their greater virtue and is a safeguard against idle talk. They may also build small churches. They should not build large ones for the purpose of preaching to the people or for any other reason. The brothers' humility is greater and their example better when they go to other churches to give sermons.

"If prelates, priests, religious or laymen should come to visit them in their places, the houses and churches will preach to them and edify them because they are small and poor."

He also said, "It often happens that the brothers have large buildings constructed. They violate our holy poverty, cause their neighbors to complain, and are a bad example to them. Later, when they can get still better and holier places, they will leave the places and buildings they have. Then the people of the locality who had made contributions and others as well, on seeing what they have done or hearing about it, will be embittered against them and be thrown into confusion. It is therefore better for the brothers to have small and very poor places and buildings built, thus remaining true to their vows and the giving of good example to their fellowmen, than going counter to their vows and giving of good example, and making a bad example for others. I mean that if it should happen that some brothers should give up their small and poor buildings when they find an opportunity of getting more worthy places, they would give very bad example, and make themselves a source of scandal."

The Saint speaks while expecting death at Siena

The brothers fear St. Francis has arrived at a final crisis
— they ask a last blessing and words of holy instruction
— a priest is called and bid to write — the brothers should
love one another, Lady Poverty, and priests — they
should beware of bad example.

In those days, and in the same cell where St.
Francis had talked with Lord Bonaventure, he
was seized one evening with a fit of vomiting
brought about by his stomach ailment. The retching
was so violent that he vomited blood. He vomited
blood all through the night and into the morning hours.
When his companions saw him brought almost to the
point of death by weakness and the pains of his illness,
they said to him, sorrowfully grieving and weeping,
"Father, what are we to do ? Bless us and your other
brothers. But leave your brothers as well some memorial
of your will so that if the Lord should want to call you
from this world, your brothers could always hold your
words fast in their memory and say, 'When our Father
was dying he left these words to his sons and brothers'."
He replied, "Call Brother Benedict of Piracro to me."
He was a brother priest; he was wise, holy, and of long
standing in the Order. Sometimes he would celebrate
Mass for St. Francis in his cell, for when he could, even
if he were ill, the holy Father would gladly and devoutly
hear Mass. When he had come, St. Francis said to him,
"Write and say that I bless all my brothers, those now

in the Order, and those who will enter it until the end of time. "

It was St. Francis's custom at the close of a Chapter to bless and absolve all the brothers gathered there along with all the other brothers in the Order, and extend his blessing to all who were to enter the Order in future times.

St. Francis continued saying, "It is hard for me to talk because I am too feeble and too tormented with the pains of my illness. So I shall make a brief declaration of my will concerning the brothers in three statements. In sign of remembrance of my blessing and my testament, they should always love and respect one another; they should always love and respect our lady, holy Poverty; and always be faithful and subject to the prelates and all the priests of Holy Mother Church. " He also admonished the brothers to fear and beware of giving bad example. Furthermore he cursed all who by their depraved and bad example should provoke men to blaspheme the Order and the brothers' way of life, and the holy and good brothers of the Order who would suffer the shame of it and be distressed.

St. Francis loves a simple Brother

Preaching near Assisi — concern for cleanliness of churches — priests are admonished out of the faithful's hearing — the story of Brother John — by exception his property is dispossessed in favor of relatives — simple John's holy imitation of St. Francis — a fleshly-minded man is rejected for giving property to relatives.

At one time, when St. Francis was dwelling at the church of St. Mary of the Portiuncula, and there were still only a few brothers, he would sometimes go to the villages and churches in the neighborhood of the city of Assisi. There he would preach and proclaim to the people that they should do penance. He would carry a broom to sweep the churches. St. Francis felt very badly about it when he would enter a church and find that it was not kept clean.

After preaching to the people he would always have any priests attending come to a retired place where the seculars would not hear. Then he would preach to the priests on the salvation of souls, but particularly he would speak to them about the painstaking care they should give to keeping clean the churches, altars, and all that pertained to the celebration of the divine mysteries.

One day St. Francis went to a church in a village belonging to the city of Assisi and began sweeping it. Soon word of his being there spread through the village, for those people liked seeing him and hearing him speak. There was a man by the name of John, an unusually simple man, who was plowing in a field he had close by the church. When he heard the news, he immediately went to look for St. Francis and found him in the church sweeping it. He said, "Brother, give me the broom; I want to help you." He took the broom and did the rest of the sweeping. When he had finished the two of them sat down, and John said to St. Francis, "For a long time I have been wanting to serve God, and I want to all the more after hearing about you and your brothers. I didn't know how to go about seeing you. Now that it has pleased the Lord to have me meet you, I want to do whatever you would like to have me do."

St. Francis rejoiced in the Lord on seeing the man's fervent piety, especially since at the time he had only a few brothers, and it seemed to him that this man would make a good Religious because of his pure simplicity. He told him, "Brother, if you want to follow our life and be one of our companions, you will have to give up everything you own, that is, all you can justly claim, as the Holy Gospel says. All my brothers who had property have done this."

When John heard this, he went straight to the field where he had left the oxen, loosed them, and led one of them to St. Francis. He said, "Brother, I have worked for my father and everyone in the household for quite a a few years. This ox is not much as a portion of my patrimony, but I want to take it for my portion and give it to the poor in any way it would seem best to you according to God."

When his parents and his brothers and sisters, who were still little children, realized that he intended leaving them, they and everyone in the house began to weep such copious tears and cry so loudly that St. Francis was moved by pity for them, especially since the family was a large one and without means to help themselves. He then said to them, " Prepare a meal and we will all sit down and eat together. Don't weep any more, because I am going to make you happy. "

With no further ado they got the meal ready and ate together in gay spirits. When they had finished eating, St. Francis told them, " This son of yours wants to serve God, and you shouldn't be sad about that; you ought to be happy about it. Not only in the eyes of God, but in the eyes of the world as well it will be looked upon as an honor for you and a good thing for your souls and bodies, because God is being honored by your flesh and blood, and all our brothers will be your sons and brothers.

" Moreover, John is a creature of God who wants to serve his Creator, and to serve God means to reign. I cannot then, nor should I, give him back to you. But so that you will have some consolation, I want him to give away the ox, but give it to you. You will be the poor to whom he gives it in this case even though the counsel of the Holy Gospel says it should be given to other poor people. "

They were all consoled by what St. Francis told them, and since they were very poor, they were especially happy about the ox being given back to them.

St. Francis had a great love for pure and holy sim-, plicity. It was something that pleased him and that he liked to find in himself and in others. Wherefore, as soon as John was clothed in a religious habit, he made him one of his companions.

Brother John was so utterly simple that he thought he was obliged to do whatever St. Francis did. So when St. Francis would be praying in a church or some secluded place, he wanted to look at him and watch him so that he could make the same movements St. Francis made. If St. Francis were to genuflect or join his hands in prayer towards heaven, Brother John would do that, and if St. Francis were to spit or cough, John would do that too.

St. Francis tried reproving him in a jolly manner for this sort of simplicity, but Brother John would answer, "Brother, I made a promise to do everything you do, and so I want to do everything you do." St. Francis thought this wonderful, and it made him happy to see so much purity and simplicity in him.

Brother John attained such heights of perfection in all virtues and good actions that St. Francis and the other brothers marveled at it. Not much time had passed before he died in that holy perfection. When St. Francis was among his brothers he would retell the things he did, rejoicing inwardly and outwardly, and when he named him he would not call him Brother John, but Saint John.

At one time St. Francis was traveling through the March country preaching. While preaching to the people of a castle town one day, a man came up to him and said, "Brother, I want to leave the world and enter your Order." "Brother," St. Francis replied, "if you want to enter the Order of the Brothers, you must first of all give all you possess to the poor, according to the perfection of the Holy Gospel, and next you must deny your own will in all things."

When the man heard this, he hastened away, and prompted by fleshly, not spiritual love, gave all his goods to his blood relations. Then he returned to St. Francis and said, "Brother, here I am, dispossessed of all I owned." St. Francis said, "How did you go about it?" He answered, "Brother, I gave away all my goods to some of my blood relations who were in need of them."

St. Francis was quick to sense that this man was fleshly-minded. He said, "Go your way, Brother Fly, you have given your goods to members of your own family, and now you expect to live with the brothers on alms." The man immediately went his way, quite unwilling to give his goods away to any other poor persons.

St. Francis in temptation

Lacking cheer during temptation he withdraws from companions — his peace is restored through a gospel message.

In those same times, St. Francis was staying at the place of St. Mary when it happened that a grievous temptation of the spirit was sent into him for the greater good of his soul. In his tribulations he even withdrew somewhat from close companionship with the brothers because he could not appear before them with his customary cheerfulness while bearing that temptation. He mortified himself, abstaining not only from food but also from speaking. Often he would go to pray in the woods near the church where he in all freedom could show his sorrow to the Lord, and weep more abundant tears before him so that the Lord, who can do all things, might deign to send him a remedy from heaven for his tribulations.

After being tormented day and night by this temptation for more than two years, he was praying one day in the church of St. Mary when these words of the Gospel were spoken within his spirit: " If you had faith as big as a mustard seed, and would tell a mountain to move from where it is and go somewhere else, that would be done (cf. *Mt* 17,20). " St. Francis replied, " What is this mountain ? " The answer given him was, " This mountain is your temptation. " St. Francis said, " Therefore, Lord, let it be done to me as you have said. " Immediately he was freed, and so completely that he was as if he had never had the temptation.

St. Francis makes amends for a leper's hurt feelings

 Lepers are called Brother Christians — in a leper's hearing St. Francis reprimands Brother James for imprudent kindness — lepers were customarily abhored — St. Francis obtains permission and does a repugnant penance.

One day when St. Francis had come back to the church of St. Mary of the Portiuncula, he found there simple Brother James with a leper who had sores and open wounds. He had come there the same day. The holy Father had warmly recommended this leper to Brother James, as he had all the lepers who were badly ulcerated.

In those days the brothers used to stay in the leper hospitals. Brother James worked like a doctor among those who had many sores and he would not hesitate to touch the wounds, change bandages and take care of them.

St. Francis in a reproving way said to Brother James, "You should not bring our Brother Christians here. It is not a good thing to do, either for you or for them." St. Francis called the lepers *Brother Christians*. Although he talked to him in this manner, he was nevertheless glad to have him assist and serve the lepers. What he objected to was having those afflicted with many sores taken out of the hospital. Brother James was extremely simple, and he would often take a leper with him to St. Mary's, for the very reason that most people abhored lepers who were badly ulcerated with sores.

105

St. Francis had no sooner said this than he was sorry for it. He went to confess his fault to Brother Peter Cattanii who at the time held the office of Minister General. He thought he had shamed the leper by rebuking Brother James. So as to make satisfaction both to God and the leper, he confessed his fault.

St. Francis said to Brother Peter, "I tell you to confirm the penance I want to do for this and be sure not to object." Brother Peter told him, "Brother, do what you think best." Brother Peter held St. Francis in such great veneration and respect, and was so obedient to him that he would not presume to change his penance, even though on this and on many other occasions it painfully distressed him inwardly and outwardly. St. Francis told him, "My penance should be this, that I eat out of the same dish with Brother Christian."

So when St. Francis sat at table with the leper and the other Brothers, a bowl was set between the two of them. Now this leper was covered with sores and open wounds. Particularly the flesh of his fingers was wasted and bloody. Whenever he put them into the bowl, blood dripped into it. On seeing this Brother Peter and the other brothers felt very badly about it, but they did not dare to say anything because of their veneration for the holy Father. He who has written this has seen it and gives testimony thereto.

Lucifer's vacant throne is reserved for St. Francis

Demons avenge St. Francis's adversary — Pacificus
mystically perceives heaven's highest throne — the
wonderfully holy St. Francis will sit there — St. Francis
humbly avows his sinfulness and confirms his sanctity.

At one time St. Francis was traveling through the
Spoleto valley and with him was Brother Pacificus who came from the March of Ancona.
In the world he had been known as King of Verses, and
had been a noble master of song in the courts. They
were given lodging in the leper hospital at Trevi. St.
Francis said to Brother Pacificus, "Let's go to St. Peter's
church at Bovara; I want to pass the night there tonight."
This church was not very far from the hospital. No one
was living there because the castle town of Trevi had
been destroyed and at the time was in ruins; few if any
people lived in the town.

When they arrived there, St. Francis told Brother
Pacificus, "You go back to the hospital. I want to stay
here alone tonight. Come back to me tomorrow morning."

When he was left by himself, he said Compline and
other prayers, and then lay down to sleep. But he could
not sleep. His spirit became fearful and he sensed diabolical suggestions. He quickly got up, went outside the
house, crossed himself, and said, "On the part of almighty God, I tell you, demons, go ahead and do whatever
harm to my body the Lord Jesus Christ has given you
power to do. I am ready to stand all you can do, because

107

my body is the greatest enemy I have. You can avenge me against my adversary and enemy." Instantly the suggestions ceased. He went back to the place he had chosen for his bed, lay down, and slept peacefully.

When morning came, Brother Pacificus returned to him. St. Francis was in prayer before the altar inside the sanctuary. Brother Pacificus stayed outside the sanctuary in front of the crucifix, and while awaiting him also prayed to the Lord.

As he prayed he was lifted up in ecstasy, *whether in or outside his body, God knows (II Cor.* 12,3), and he perceived many thrones in heaven. He saw that one of them was higher than the others. It was glorious and resplendent, ornamented with precious stones in great variety. While admiring its beauty he began to wonder what sort of throne it could be, and whose it was. Suddenly he heard a voice telling him, "This was Lucifer's throne, and in his stead, St. Francis will sit upon it." He had barely returned to his senses when St. Francis came out to him. Straightway he threw himself down at the feet of the holy Father and lay in the form of a cross on the floor. Still under the influence of the vision he had just seen, he thought St. Francis was already in heaven.

He said, "Father, forgive my sins and pray the Lord to forgive me and have mercy on me." St. Francis stretched out his hand and lifted him up, knowing that he had seen something while he was praying. Brother Pacificus saw him as if wholly transformed, and spoke to him as one not living in the flesh, but already reigning in Heaven.

After a while and in an unconcerned manner, since he did not want to speak of his vision to St. Francis, he asked him, "What opinion do you have of yourself, brother?" St. Francis replied, "In my opinion I am more sinful than any other man in the world." Thereupon it was told Brother Pacificus in spirit, "By this you know that your vision was true, for just as Lucifer was cast out of that throne because of his pride, just so will St. Francis merit being exalted and made to sit upon it because of his humility."

The singular meeting of Pacificus with St. Francis

Pacificus as a mundane celebrity feels an urge to meet St. Francis — he recognizes the Saint and his genuine holiness by a glowing *Thau* — he demands a deed and is clothed as a brother — interpretation of a *Thau* composed of peacock feathers.

At one time St. Francis was traveling through the March of Ancona. As yet Brother Pacificus had not known him, and had never seen his face. He had merely heard about him through his fame that spread as if winged by birds far and wide. He was still a man who prized and craved the vanity of mundane glamor. However, the fact that he was being pressed on by eager desire and was going in all haste to find the Saint was a presage of the grace which with the passing of time he was to acquire.

109

As he drew near he saw St. Francis for the first time. He was standing among the other brothers, just as one of them. By discernment given him by God he knew which one was St. Francis, because the Lord pointed him out. He had placed over his head a *Thau* that was like a shining emblem radiating beams of light. By that sign Pacificus was made to know clearly that here was a man who practiced penance with genuine, heartfelt grief, and was a true minister of the Word of God which is like a sharp sword severing man's fleshliness from him, and a refulgent light illuminating his soul. Pacificus stood there not saying a word, gazing with wonder at the sign granted him, by divine pleasure, of St. Francis's eminent holiness.

As was his custom, St. Francis preached on contempt of the world, with arguments against worldly pomp. He directed his preaching to the man he saw before him who most brazenly displayed signs of worldly conceit. Pacificus, not yet a brother, was pierced by the sword of God's word. He spoke and made a reply to St. Francis saying, "I need your deeds more than your words." St. Francis replied, "Well, what do you want me to do for you?" Pacificus said, "I want you to give me your tunic."

The holy Father did not fail to grant his pious request. He gave him his tunic, and in giving it clothed him in the habit of the Order. In this garb he did praiseworthy combat until he brought his life to a still more praiseworthy end.

After the brother had taken the habit and was ac-

110

companying him on one occasion, he once again saw the sign *Thau* above St. Francis. It had the appearance of being made of peacock feathers. By this sign it was clearly shown that St. Francis was generously ornamented with *God's manifold grace* (cf. *I Pt* 4,10).

The Saint's teaching on work and disciplined speech

> Work is a remedy for laziness — through idle talk graces gained are lost — provisions for the discipline of speech — a prayer said on entering the company of other Brothers.

henever our very holy father Francis stayed at St. Mary of the Portiuncula, it was his practice on any day he was there to do some work with the brothers after mealtime as a means of counteracting the vice of laziness. He thought that in this way the brothers would not lose the good gained, with God's help, in the time they spent in prayer, but which could be lost through idle and useless speech. So as to avoid this evil, he established the following rulings:

If a brother, when traveling or busy with some kind of work, should talk to the brothers about idle or useless things, he must say one *Our Father*, praising God at the beginning and the end of this prayer, but according to certain conditions. If it is the offending brother who first becomes aware of his fault and accuses himself, he

111

says the *Our Father* for his own soul along with the *Praises of God* as stated above. If however another brother first makes the accusation, the offender must say the *Our Father* in the above-stated manner, but for the brother making the accusation. If upon being accused he makes excuses for himself and will not say the *Our Father*, he must say the *Our Father* twice in the above-stated manner for the soul of the brother who has accused him, provided that by the latter's testimony, or that of another brother, it is verified that the brother has actually thus spoken. He must say the *Praises of God*, as has been stated, before and after the prayer, in a voice loud and clear enough to be heard and understood by the brothers present. These brothers must remain silent and listen. If a brother should act in a sense contrary to the ruling, and should not keep silent, he must say one *Our Father* together with the *Praises of God* in the same manner as is stated above, for the soul of the other brother who was saying the prayer.

When a brother enters the cell, the house, or any of the places, and finds there a brother or brothers, he must on each such occasion devoutly praise and bless God.

It was always the holy Father's custom to say these *Praises*, and he ardently desired that the brothers, as well as other people, should say them attentively and devoutly.

The brothers are sent to foreign countries

At a Chapter it is decided to send brothers abroad —
St. Francis assumes the duty of being example — after
prayer he chooses France because of devotion to the
Eucharist in that country — his instructions on care
of the Blessed Sacrament — instructions on behavior
of brothers accompanying him on his journey.

At a Chapter celebrated at that same place, brothers were for the first time sent to lands beyond
the seas. At the end of the Chapter, St. Francis
remained at that place with some of the brothers. He
told them, "My very dear brothers, it is my duty to be
the model and example for all the brothers. Therefore,
now that I have sent my brothers to distant lands to
labor, and bear shame, hunger, and many other hardships,
it seems to me just and good that I too go to some distant
country. When they hear that I am enduring all they
endure, they will have the courage to bear their want
and hardships with greater patience."

Then he told them, "Go therefore and pray to the
Lord. Ask him to grant me the grace to choose the
country which best serves his glory, the benefit and
salvation of souls, and the good example of our Order."

It was the holy Father's custom to pray to the Lord
and have the brothers pray that the Lord would direct
his heart and that he would travel to whatever country
was best in God's eyes. He did this not only when setting
out to preach in a distant land, but also when going
to preach in the country nearby.

113

The brothers prayed and then came back to him. He told them, "In the name of our Lord Jesus Christ and his glorious Virgin Mother and all the saints, I choose the land of France. In that country the people are Catholic, and they are the most outstanding of all Catholics of the holy Church in their devotion to the Body of Christ. This is a devotion I like very much, and on this account I will the more gladly deal with them."

St. Francis had such great reverence and devotion for the Body of Christ that he wanted it written in the rule that the brothers should be carefully attentive in this matter wherever they were living, and he admonished them that they should preach about it to clerics and priests, telling them to reserve the Body of Christ in a fitting and worthy place. If the brothers should find that they were not doing so, they should then take care of it themselves.

At one time he sent some brothers with ciboria to all the provinces. Wherever they found the Body of Christ being reserved unbefittingly they were to place it honorably in one of these.

Likewise, because of his reverence for the most holy Body and Blood of the Lord Jesus Christ, he had wanted a statement put in the rule regarding those written words or names of the Lord through which the Holy Sacrament is effected. If the brothers should ever come upon such written words not kept in a proper place, or left disrespectfully lying about, they should gather them up and put them in a suitable place, and thus honor the Lord in the words he has spoken.

114

Many are the things which are sanctified by the words of God and by virtue of the words of Christ by which the Sacrament of the altar is effected. Actually the directives were not written in the rule because the Brother Ministers held that the brothers should not be bound to these things by force of command. Yet the holy Father did express his will in these matters in his *Testament* and in other writings.

He sent other brothers to all the provinces with good and well-made irons for making hosts.

St. Francis chose brothers whom he wanted to take with him from among the brothers attending the Chapter. He gave them these instructions: "In the name of the Lord, go two by two in a decorous way along the road and keep silence from early morning until after the Hour of Tierce, praying silently in your hearts to the Lord. Let no idle or useless word be mentioned among you. Even though you are walking along the road, let your conversation be no less virtuous than it would be if you were in your hermitage or cell.

"No matter where we are, or where we might be traveling, we have our cell along with us. Brother Body is the cell, and the soul is a hermit dwelling in it. There it prays to God and meditates. To be sure, if the soul does not have quiet and solitude in the cell where it dwells, the cell made by hands will not profit the Religious very much."

The demons are driven out of Arezzo

Demons foment strife among the people of Arezzo —
St. Francis has Brother Sylvester exorcise the city —
peace is restored — the ungrateful people return to
service of the demons.

When they arrived at Arezzo, practically the whole
city was seething with strife. The people were
divided by long-standing hatred between two
factions and were battling each other day and night.

St. Francis was lodged at a hospice in a suburb outside
the city. He was convinced that the demons were enjoying
their triumph and were goading the people on to the
destruction of their own city, burning the buildings down
and ruining it in other fearful ways. He felt pity for the
city and said to Brother Sylvester, a priest, a man of
God, strong in faith, of great simplicity and purity, and
whom the holy Father venerated as a saint, "Go and
stand before the gate of the city. Shout good and loud,
and order the demons to get out of the city."

Brother Sylvester went then to the city gate. Standing
there he shouted in a loud voice, "The Lord Jesus Christ
be blessed and praised! On behalf of almighty God and
by virtue of holy obedience to our very holy father Francis,
I order all demons to get out of this city."

Then it came to pass by divine mercy and the prayer
of St. Francis, even though no preaching had been done,
that peace and unity were restored to the people of that
city.

116

St. Francis could not preach to them at that time. But on a later occasion he did preach to them. He told them in his first sermon, "I speak to you as to slaves of demons. You have bound yourselves like wretches to the demons. You have sold yourselves to them like beasts in the market place and put yourselves right into their hands. You did this when you submitted to the will of the men who have destroyed and are still destroying both themselves and you, and who are bent upon destroying your whole city. What a wretched and ignorant people you are when you are ungrateful for God's gifts! Maybe some of you do not know it, but at a certain hour God liberated this city through the merits of the very holy Brother Sylvester."

The Bishop of Ostia forbids St. Francis's journey to France

St. Francis meets the Bishop of Ostia at Florence — opposition to St. Francis in the Roman Curia requires his presence in Italy — he justifies the hardships suffered by brothers in foreign lands — the brothers have a universal vocation.

When St. Francis arrived at Florence, he went to see the Lord Hugolin, Bishop of Ostia, who was later to become pope. He was there because Pope Honorius had appointed him papal legate for the Duchy of Spoleto, Tuscany, Lombardy, and the March of Treviso as far as the Venetian border. The Lord Bishop was overjoyed to welcome St. Francis at Florence. However, when St. Francis told him his intention of going to France, the Lord Bishop forbade him to go there. He said, "Brother, it is not my will that you go to any country beyond the mountains. At Rome there are a number of prelates and other persons who would be glad to oppose your interests at the Roman Curia. I and other Cardinals have your Order at heart, and we are more than willing to protect it and give it our support. You though must stay within the confines of this country." St. Francis answered, "Lord, it would be a shameful thing for me, if after sending my brothers to far away places in distant lands I should stay here in this country." To this the Lord Bishop answered in a tone of reproof, "But why did you send your Brothers so far away to starve and face all kinds of hardships?"

St. Francis was transported by the Spirit and prophetically declared, "Is it your idea, or do you believe that the Lord sent the brothers to serve only the people of these lands? I tell you truly that the Lord chose the brothers and sent them for the good and the salvation of all souls everywhere in the world. They will be received in lands of the faithful and in lands of the infidels as well. As long as they fulfill what they have promised the Lord; he will take care of their needs whether they be in the lands of the infidels or of the faithful."

The Lord Bishop's admiration was aroused by his words, and he affirmed that what St. Francis said was the truth. Nevertheless, he did not grant St. Francis permission for the trip. St. Francis sent Brother Pacificus with some other brothers to France, while he returned to the Spoleto valley.

St. Francis explains his conscience as superior

On the eve of a Chapter St. Francis tells a companion what his attitude is on his office — whether reviled or praised he has cause for joy.

Once when a Chapter of the brothers was about to be held at the church of St. Mary of the Portiuncula, St. Francis told his companion, "In my opinion I'm not a Lesser Brother unless I am in a situation I'm going to describe for you." He then went on to say, "Suppose that the brothers are coming here to me. They show signs of devotion and veneration, and they invite me to the Chapter. I am touched by their warm devotion, and I go with them to attend the Chapter. They assemble and call upon me to announce the word of God to them. I get up and preach as the Holy Spirit teaches me to preach. Suppose now the sermon is ended. They think it over and complain, telling me, 'You're not an eloquent speaker and we don't want you governing us. In fact, we're ashamed of you. What a simple, despicable person you are to have as a superior! Let this be clear: from now on don't presume to call yourself our superior!' Then they put me out of the Chapter meeting, shouting insults after me.

"I don't think I would be a Lesser Brother if I were not just as happy with their vilification and the shame of their casting me out, and not wanting me as superior any more, as I was when they treated me with honor and veneration, and if I did not think that as far as they are concerned, they are just as well off whether I am their superior or whether I am not.

"If I enjoy having their support and receiving their honor, after all dangerous for my soul, there is still greater cause for rejoicing in the good they do me and the benefit to my soul's salvation when they revile and shame me by casting me out, for in this treatment there is gain for my soul."

Sister Locust sings for St. Francis

A locust delights the Saint by singing at his bidding — he gives her permission to depart for fear of flattering his vanity.

At one time during the summer, St. Francis was staying at that same place in the last cell near the hedge of the garden behind the house. Brother Rainerius, the gardener, lived there after the Saint had died.

On coming out of the cell one day, there happened to be a locust on the branch of a fig tree growing beside his cell, and it was perched at a place where he could reach it. He stretched his hand out to it and said, "Come to me, my Sister Locust." Thereupon, it crawled onto the fingers of his hand and he stroked it with a finger of the other hand while telling it, "Sing, my Sister Locust!"

It immediately obeyed him and sang. This pleased St. Francis very much, and he praised God. He kept it on his hand for a good hour, and then put it back on the branch of the fig tree from which he had taken it. For the following eight days he would find it perched at that same place when coming out of his cell, and each day he would take it on his hand. When he stroked it and told it to sing, then it would sing. On the eighth day he said to his companions, "We should grant Sister Locust permission to go wherever she likes. She has given us pleasure enough. The flesh could take vainglory in this."

No sooner had he given his permission than it went off and was never seen there again. His companions marveled, because it obeyed him like this and was so tame in his hands.

St. Francis took such great delight in creatures for the love of their Creator, that the Lord cheered him inwardly and outwardly by making tame for him the creatures that are naturally wild for other men.

The Saint chooses good example instead
of warm clothing

St. Francis sews pieces of cloth inside his habit for warmth — remembering the duty of good example he removes them.

At one time St. Francis was staying at the hermitage of St. Eleutherius near a certain castle town called Contigliano in the county of Rieti. He had brought only one tunic with him. One day it was so very cold, and he was in such great need of warmer clothing that he took his tunic, and his companion's as well, and patched it on the inside with pieces of cloth so that he could warm his body up a bit. Not long afterwards, he came out from the place where he had been praying and said very joyfully to his companion, "It is my duty to be a model and example for all the brothers. True, I need these pieces of cloth under my tunic, but it is also true that I must keep my brothers in mind. They need the same thing, and perhaps some don't have the cloth and can't get it. In consideration of them, it is my duty to suffer the privations they suffer. When they hear about what I do, they will be able to suffer their trials with greater patience."

How great and how many needs he denied his body by way of food and clothing so as to give good example, and so that the other brothers could bear their privations with greater patience, is something that we who were with him would never be able to tell. St. Francis always gave first and foremost attention to this practice, after the brothers had begun to multiply and he had resigned his office as superior, in order that his deeds might teach them better than his words what they should do and what they should refrain from doing.

The Lord not St. Francis rules the Order

St. Francis suffers keenly because of defecting friars — the Lord enlightens him: he has called the brothers and he gives the strength to persevere — he chose St. Francis to preside over his family not because of ability but because of simplicity — defecting brothers lose grace gained — the Lord will sustain the Order until the end of time.

One time St. Francis was pained to the very depths of his heart because of news coming to his ears about brothers who had given bad example in the Order, even defecting and descending from the lofty heights of their vows.

While in prayer one day he said to the Lord, "Lord, I give back into your hands the family you gave me." The Lord then spoke within him and said, "Tell me, why does it make you so extremely sad when a brother leaves the Order, or when the brothers do not walk by the way I showed you ? And tell me this: Who planted the Order of the Brothers ? Who is it that brings about

123

a man's conversion so that he will want to do penance in the Order ? Who gives him the strength to persevere in it ? Is it not I ?"

It was also told him in spirit, "Do you think I chose you and placed you over my family because you were educated and eloquent ? I chose you because you were simple and insomuch could know, both you and the others, that it is I who watch over my flock. I placed you as a seal upon them (cf. *Hg* 2,23) so that they could see the works I do in you and then do likewise. Those who walk in the way I showed you have me, and have me abundantly. Those who will not walk on my way will have what they think they have taken away from them (cf. *Mt* 25,29). Therefore, I tell you, do not grieve so much. Instead, just do what you do, and work at your work, because I have planted the Order of the Brothers in never-ending love (*Jer* 31,3). You may know this, that my love for the Order is so great that if one brother should return to his vomit (cf. *II Pt* 2,22) and die outside the Order, I will place another man in the Order, and he will receive the other's crown. If that man is not yet born, then I shall have him born.

"So that you will know that I love the life and Order of the brothers with a whole heart, I give you this assurance: even if there were just a handful of brothers left in the whole life and Order of the brothers, I would, until the end of time, not forsake it."

St. Francis's obligations to the Order after resignation

He will not intervene in case of abuses — since the obligation of the rule is accepted by all alike under vow, his own example and his prayer must suffice.

After these words had been spoken in his spirit, St. Francis was greatly consoled, for he had always been extremely pained when he heard of brothers giving bad example. Henceforth he was . so fortified by the Lord that although he could not help but be saddened on hearing bad news about his brothers, he could keep from giving way to sorrow by recalling this incident and talking about it with his companions.

Often St. Francis would say to the brothers when speaking to them in the Chapters or when giving them spiritual talks, "I have sworn and resolved to observe the rule of the brothers and they have all bound themselves under the same obligation. Consequently, now that I have resigned my office as their superior for reason of illness and for the good of my soul and the souls of all the brothers, I am held to no further duty in their regard than the giving of good example. I have been informed by the Lord, and know it to be true, that even if I were not excused by illness, the greatest assistance I can give the Order of the Brothers is in going to pray to the Lord for it each day, and asking him to govern, sustain, protect, and defend it.

"In this regard, I have assumed an obligation to the Lord and to the brothers; namely, if a brother should perish through any bad example of mine, I want to be held accountable for it by the Lord."

At times a brother would suggest that he intervene in the affairs of the Order. His answer would be: "The brothers have their rule, and they have moreover sworn to uphold it. So that they might have no excuse, after it had pleased the Lord to place me over them as superior, I made the same oath in their presence, and it is my will to observe it to the end. Since the brothers know what they ought to do, and what they must refrain from doing, there is nothing left for me to do but teach them by my deeds. For this I was given to them while I live, and after my death."

An example of St. Francis's earnest faithfulness to poverty

For love of Lady Poverty, and because of his vow he should be poorer than paupers.

At one time when St. Francis was traveling about in a certain country to preach, he came upon a man who was desperately poor. Seeing how poverty-stricken the man was, he said to his companion, "We are badly shamed by this man's poverty; it is a reproach to our poverty." His companion asked, "How is that, brother?" He explained, "It makes me very ashamed when I find a man who is poorer than myself.

I chose holy poverty as my lady, as my delight and my riches of spirit and body. Word of what I have done has resounded far and wide. Everybody knows I have made a vow of poverty before God and man. I can then only be ashamed when I come upon a man who is still poorer than I am. "

The mirror of the Incarnate Christ

St. Francis gives a penance to a brother who has spoken unkindly of an ailing pauper — the pauper has come in the name of Christ who assumed poverty and infirmity for our salvation.

At one time while preaching to the people in the country around Rocca di Bricio, he stayed in a hermitage near the town. On the day he was going to preach at that place, a very poor and sickly man came to him. When St. Francis saw him, he pitied him because he was so very poor and in such bad health. He spoke compassionately to his companion about how naked and sickly the man was. The companion remarked, "Brother, it is true that the man is awfully poor, but it could be that no one in the whole country has a greater desire to be rich."

St. Francis rebuked him for his unkind remark, and the companion admitted his fault. The holy Father then said, "Do you want to do the penance I'll tell you to do?" The companion answered, "I would be glad to." Thereupon he told his companion, "Go and take off your tunic, go up to that poor man naked, and throw yourself down at his feet. Tell him how you have sinned against him by belittling him, and ask him to pray God for your forgiveness."

The companion went and did exactly what St. Francis had told him, got up, put on his tunic, and came back. Then St. Francis said, "Do you want me to explain how you sinned against that man, and in fact against Christ himself?" He went on to say, "When you see a poor man you should turn your thoughts to the One in whose name he has come, I mean to Christ. Christ came taking upon himself our poverty and infirmity. This man's poverty and infirmity is a mirror to reflect Christ for us. We should look with piety at his image and see there the poverty and infirmity our Lord Jesus Christ took upon himself and bore in his body for mankind's salvation."

St. Francis reads a brother's secret thoughts

The Saint perceives what a longsuffering brother does not tell him about boorish treatment — the overbearing offender leaves the Order.

At one time, a brother whom St. Francis held in warm affection traveled northward from Terra Laboris, which is the region around Caserta, with another brother who was his senior in religion. The latter was often angry with his companion and quarreled with him. His fits of anger were altogether unjustified for the younger brother was in no way at fault. He nevertheless bore the abuse without complaining.

They arrived at a certain place where St. Francis lay ill at the time, and the brother who was St. Francis's friend went into his cell. While talking to him about various things, St. Francis asked the brother, "How did your companion treat you while you were traveling with him?" The brother answered, "Father, very well." The Saint said, "Now be careful. You could lie to me under pretext of being humble. I know how he behaved with you."

The brother marveled greatly because the holy Father had known through the Holy Spirit what he had not told him or anybody else. It so happened that shortly afterwards the quarrelsome brother left the Order.

St. Francis perceives a brother's state of soul

He frees a brother from a temptation which the brother had not mentioned to him.

There was a brother of holy and virtuous life and constant in prayer who had entered the Order among the first brothers. For a number of years he was tempted by different kinds of strong temptations. He was so sorely tried by them that oftentimes he mortified himself severely by practicing abstinence, making long vigils, shedding tears, and praying. He could get no relief nor remedy from within himself or from any of his brothers. He wanted to see St. Francis to get his counsel.

While walking along a road, by divine dispensation, he came upon St. Francis who was traveling through that country to preach. When he recognized him, he ran to him, threw himself down at his feet, and wept so bitterly that he was unable to speak a word. St. Francis felt great pity for him, and instantly knew through the Holy Spirit that he was being tormented by a grievous temptation. He said, "In the name of our Lord Jesus Christ, I command you, demons, to desist this minute from molesting my brother as you have been doing until now." Immediately the brother arose and found himself so totally liberated that he was as if he had never had the temptation.

St. Francis comprehends Brother Bandits

The brothers have a problem: should they or should they not be merciful to evil men ? — St. Francis tells the brothers how to be merciful and correct the evil of the men — the fraternal charity gains the conversion of dangerous bandits.

At one time there were bandits who came sometimes to the hermitage located above Borgo San Sepolcro and begged bread from the brothers. These bandits lived in hiding in the vast forests of the region. From time to time they would venture onto the open highways and roads to rob and despoil the people.

One brother of the place said, "It is not right to give them alms. They're thieves and do a lot of harm to the people." Other brothers took into account that when the bandits asked for bread they were humble about it, and that they were driven by desperate need. They would give them something, but not without admonishing them to convert and do penance.

St. Francis came to the place during this time. The brothers asked him whether they should give bread to the bandits or not. St. Francis said, "If you do as I tell you, I can trust the Lord to enrich their souls." He then told them, "Go and get some good bread and some good wine, and take them into the forest where you know they live. Then shout out these words: 'Brother Bandits, come here! We are brothers and we've brought you some good bread and some good wine!' They'll come right away. Then spread a tablecloth on the ground, set the bread and wine on it, and serve them humbly and cheerfully while they eat. When they've finished eating, talk to them about our Lord's teachings. Finish by asking them to grant a first request for love of the Lord. They should promise you that they will not strike anyone nor injure anyone's person. Don't ask them to promise everything at one time, because they wouldn't grant it. Because you have treated them humbly and charitably, they'll promise you this much right away.

"Then go again another day. In consideration of their goodness in making a promise to you, add eggs and cheese to the bread and wine. Bring them the food and serve them as you did before until they have finished eating. Then tell them, '*Why do you stand there the whole day* (cf. *Mt* 20,6) ? Here you are dying of hunger and you suffer all kinds of hardships, while by your will and your actions you do many wicked deeds. At the end you will have to pay for it with the loss of your souls unless you be converted (cf. *Ps* 7,13). It would be better for you to serve the Lord. Do this and he will grant you your needs in this life, and at the end he will save your souls'. The Lord will thereupon, in his mercy, inspire them to convert because you have treated them with humility and charity. "

So the brothers went and did everything St. Francis had told them to do. Through God's mercy and his grace coming upon them, each of the brothers' demands was accepted and observed, point by point. In appreciation of the friendship and charity the brothers had shown them, they brought loads of wood on their backs to the hermitage. In fact, by the mercy of God they responded so willingly to the brothers' charity and friendship, that some entered the Order and others became penitents. In this manner they made their promises in the hands of the brothers to commit no more evil deeds but live by the work of their hands.

The brothers and the people who heard about what had happened marveled at this sign of St. Francis's holiness. He had predicted the conversion of these men who had been so malicious and evil and their conversion to the Lord had come about quickly.

An innocent lamb's death is avenged

A sow kills a newborn lamb — St. Francis bewails innocence thus maltreated — he invokes punishment of the offending sow and its delectable flesh is disdained.

At one time St. Francis was a guest for a night at the monastery of St. Verecundius in the diocese of Gubbio. That night an ewe gave birth to a lambkin in a barn nextdoor to the house where St. Francis slept, and that same night a sow in the barn killed it.

In the morning the men of the monastery awoke and found the little lamb dead. They were quite sure the sow had done the killing and remarked as much one to another. St. Francis heard what they were saying, and it moved him to pity the poor lambkin. Before the monks and the men of the monastery he cried out, "Oh, brother mine, little lamb, such an innocent animal and so useful to men, and you always go bleating and proclaiming '*good*' (b-e-n-e)!" Then he declared, "For this may the sow that killed you be so cursed that no man, beast, or bird will eat of it!"

By divine dispensation, the sow took sick and within three days was dead. It was thrown into the ditch surrounding the monastery. What the holy Father had predicted was verified to the letter because it lay there for a long time, whole and entire.

The monks and the men of the monastery marveled exceedingly at this sign of St. Francis's holiness. They believed this a great miracle, and declared it to be such to the brothers and other people.

St. Francis perceives guile behind the pious appearances of a brother

A brother gains admiration by singular asceticism —
St. Francis recommends that willingness to confess be
made a test — the hypocritical brother has an evil end.

There was a brother who led a virtuous and holy life, and was very conscientious about praying both day night. He observed silence so consistently that there were times when he would confess to a brother priest by making signs instead of speaking. He appeared to be sincerely devout and fervent in his love of God, because sometimes when sitting with the brothers, although not saying a word, he would manifest inner and outer joy at hearing something virtuous talked about. Indeed, the devotion to God of all the brothers and other folk as well was aroused at the sight of his example. They were all convinced he was a saint.

He had been living this sort of life for a number of years when St. Francis came to the place where he lived. When he heard what the brothers had to say about this brother's mode of life, he said, "You may know that this is a case of diabolical temptation and deception because the brother doesn't want to confess."

In the meantime, the Minister General came to the place to visit St. Francis, and he too spoke of the brother in terms of praise. St. Francis told him, "Believe me, brother, this brother has been led on and deceived by an evil spirit." The Minister General answered, "It would seem to me very strange, and an almost incredible thing if you could be right about this brother. He gives so many signs of holiness and does so many saintly deeds." St. Francis then said, "Test him. Tell him he must go to confession twice, or at least once a week. If he will not agree to it, you will know that what I have told you is the truth."

One day the Minister General talked to the brother, and told him, "Brother, it is my decided will that you go twice or at least once a week to confession." The brother placed his finger on his lips, shook his head, and signified that he would by no means do it. The Minister, fearing to start a quarrel, let him go away.

Not many days had passed before the brother, of his own will, left the Order. He returned to the world where he wore secular clothing. It happened that two of St. Francis's companions were walking along the road one day when they came upon him walking alone and looking like a penniless vagabond.

They spoke to him compassionately and said, "Oh wretched fellow, where now is your holy way of life and your virtue? You cherished your solitary life so much you wouldn't mix with the brothers and talk with them. Now you go wandering hither and thither about the country like a man who knows neither God nor his servants."

The man then talked to them, and in talking would swear by saying "by my faith!" as is the way of worldly men. The brothers said to him, "Wretched man, why do you swear 'by my faith' like a worldly man when you talk? How can you do this when you were once a Religious and refused not only to speak idle words, but even good ones?"

His answer was, "I can't help it." They took leave of him in this state, and in this state he died soon afterwards.

The brothers and other folk marveled greatly at this sign of St. Francis's holiness because he had predicted the silent brother's fall at a time when the brothers and everybody else believed he was a saint.

An angel plays music for St. Francis

St. Francis laments the abuse of musical instruments — he asks a brother to borrow a zither to accompany the singing of the *Canticle of Brother Sun* — fearing scandal the brother is reluctant — an angel plays a zither to console St. Francis in tribulation.

At one time St. Francis was at Rieti for the cure of his eye disease; he was lodged there in a room of Tabaldus the Saracen's house. One day he said to one of his companions who had been a zither player in the world, "Brother, the sons of this world don't understand divine things. In ancient times musical

136

instruments, such as zithers, ten-stringed psalteries, and other instruments were used by saintly men for praising God and consoling souls. People now make a vain usage of them, and play on them in such a way as to sin against the Lord's will. So I would like you to go in secret and get a zither from some pious man, then use it to play some virtuous music for me. We will sing the verses of the *Praises of the Lord* to it, for my body is suffering very badly from sickness and pain. If we do this I can turn my bodily pain into spiritual joy and consolation.

St. Francis had composed some *Praises of the Lord* during his illness, and at times would have his companions sing them in praise of the Lord and to cheer his own soul and sometimes to edify others.

The brother answered, "Father, I would be ashamed to go for it. The people in this city know I was a zither player in the world. I am afraid they would suspect I was being tempted to do zither playing again." St. Francis said, "That being the case, brother, we shall do without it."

During the night at about midnight, St. Francis was lying awake when he heard beautiful strains of music being played near the house on a zither. It was the most delightful music he had ever heard in his life. The zither player would withdraw as far away as he could and still be heard, then he would come back, the whole time playing on his zither. He kept on doing this for a good hour. St. Francis believed this was God's work and not man's. He was filled with joy, and with an exulting heart he praised with all his might the Lord who with such and so much consolation had deigned to console him.

When he awoke in the morning, he said to his companion, "I asked it of you, brother, and you did not do what I wanted, but the Lord who consoles his friends in tribulation deigned this night to console me." He then told him all that had happened.

The brothers marveled for they believed this a great miracle. They knew it was truly a work of God for St. Francis's consolation because not only at midnight, but at no time after the third tolling of the bell would anyone venture out in the city, for the mayor had issued orders prohibiting it. Furthermore it must have been a work of God because, as St. Francis said, the zither player in going back and forth did so silently, speaking no word, nor making any sound whatsoever with his mouth.

A miraculous vintage rewards a priest's forbearance

Ecclesiastic dignitaries trample vines and eat grapes when visiting St. Francis at St. Fabian's — St. Francis calms the priest proprietor with a promise — the wine crop exceeds the vineyard's possibilities.

During this same time, St. Francis stayed at the church of St. Fabian near the same city where he had gone to have his eye disease taken care of. A poor secular priest lived at that church. The Lord Pope Honorius was in the city at the time, accompanied by some Cardinals. A number of the Cardinals and other clerics came almost daily to visit the holy Father for they held him in devout reverence.

A small vineyard belonging to the church was located beside the house where St. Francis was staying. There was only one door in the house and all the visitors came in through the vineyard. It was the season when the grapes were ripe, and it was a pleasant place to pass the time and rest. There were some of the visitors who found it agreeable to pick grapes and eat them there, while others liked to pick them and take them away. Still others trampled down the vines.

This upset the priest and made him angry. He declared, " This year I have lost my wine crop. It is true that my vineyard is just a little one, but I get enough wine from it for what I need. " When St. Francis heard about the situation, he asked to have the priest called to him. He told him, " Don't let yourself get upset and angry; there is nothing we can do about it. Instead, put your trust in the Lord, for he can make restitution for the damage in my stead. Tell me: how many measures did you get when your vintage produced the most ? " The priest told him, " Father, thirteen measures. " St. Francis replied, " Don't let the matter bother you at all; don't speak harsh words to anybody, and don't quarrel. Trust the Lord and my words. If the measures of wine you get turn out to be less than twenty, I shall see to it that the difference is made up for. " The priest was calmed by what St. Francis said, and he kept quiet about the matter.

It turned out that by divine dispensation he got

twenty measures and no less, just as St. Francis had said. The priest marveled at this as did everyone else who heard about it. They believed it was a great miracle worked through the merits of St. Francis. Indeed even if the vineyard had not been ruined, and if it had been loaded with grapes and none carried away, in the opinion of the priest and other people, it would have been impossible to get twenty measures of wine from it. Therefore, we who were with him give testimony about him, because each time he said "something is or is going to be thus" so would it be. We have seen many such words of his fulfilled during his lifetime and after his death.

A fine meal is served to St. Francis's doctor

The Saint tells the brothers to invite the doctor to a good meal — they are embarrassed by their poor fare — St. Francis wants obedience in faith — the fine meal is providentially supplied.

During this same time, St. Francis stayed at the hermitage of the brothers of Fonte Colombo near Rieti where he had gone to have his eye disease taken care of. One day the eye doctor of that city visited him and remained with him for some hours as he usually did. When he was ready to leave, St. Francis said to one of his companions, "Go and give the doctor a fine meal." The companion answered, "Father, we are ashamed to say that we're so poor that it would be very embarrassing to invite him to a meal right now and give him something to eat." St. Francis said to his companions, "Oh you of little faith! Don't make me say anything more." The doctor said to St. Francis and his companions, "Brother, I would be all the more willing to eat with the brothers because they are so poor." He was a very rich man, and often when St. Francis and his companions invited him, he would not stay to eat with them.

The brothers went and prepared the table, and much embarrassed, placed before him the little bread and wine they had with the few vegetables they had got ready for themselves. They sat down at the table, and had hardly begun to eat when there was a knock on the door of the hermitage. One of the brothers went to the door and opened it. There stood a woman carrying a large basket filled with fine bread, fishes, shrimp patties, honey and some grapes as good as if freshly cut. The lady of a castle located about seven miles away from the hermitage had sent these things.

When the brothers and the doctor saw this, they marveled greatly at the evidence of St. Francis's holiness. The doctor remarked about it to the brothers saying, "My brothers, neither you nor we realize as we ought how holy this saint is!"

Remember Scott's cheesecake

141

St. Francis reconciles a cruel husband with his wife and the Lord

St. Francis is kind and gentle to a wearied noble lady — she is distressed because a cruel husband forbids service to the Lord — his message to the husband results in his conversion and new love of his wife — the two are sanctified by chastity and good works.

One day St. Francis was traveling to the Celle di Cortona. While passing along the road beneath a castle town called Lisciano, near the brothers' place at Preggio, a noblewoman, the lady of the castle, came hastening toward St. Francis, wanting to have a talk with him. One of his companions noticed her and saw that her walking and hurrying had exhausted her. He ran to St. Francis and told him, "Father, for the love of God, let us wait for this lady. She's all tired out, and she's coming after us because she wants to talk with you."

St. Francis, a man of great charity and piety, stopped and waited for her. He saw how wearied she was, and with what fervor and devotion she was coming to him. He said, "What is it you wish, my lady?" The woman answered, "Please bless me, Father." St. Francis asked her, "Are you married or single?" She replied, "Father, it is a long time now since the Lord bestowed upon me a strong will to serve him. I have had, as I still have, a great desire to save my soul, but my husband is a cruel man. He objects to either of us serving Christ. My soul is so afflicted by pain and anguish that I could die."

St. Francis saw that her spirit was extremely ardent, but that she was just a girl, and physically delicate. He was moved by pity for her. He blessed her, and said, "Go now. You will find your husband at home. Tell him on my behalf that I ask both him and you, for the love of the Lord who endured the suffering of the Cross for our salvation, to save your souls. You should though continue to live at your home."

She went back and entered the house. There she found her husband at home as St. Francis had said. Her husband asked her, "Where have you been?" She replied, "I have been to see St. Francis, and he blessed me. My soul has been consoled and it rejoices in the Lord. He also told me to tell you on his behalf, that while continuing to live at home we should save our souls."

As she said this, the grace of God descended upon him through the merits of St. Francis. He answered her in a kind and mild way for he had been swiftly transformed by the Lord. "Lady," he said, "from now on we shall serve Christ and save our souls as St. Francis said." His wife then said, "My lord, it seems to me that it would be a good thing to live in chastity. It is something very pleasing to God, and is a virtue highly recompensed." Her husband answered, "Lady, it pleases me because it pleases you. In this and in other good works, I want my will to be at one with your will."

Thereafter they lived in chastity, and continued to do so for many years, while giving generous alms to the brothers and to other poor people. Their sanctity gained the admiration not only of the layfolk, but of the Religious too, and especially since that man who had so suddenly become spiritual had formerly been extremely worldly-minded.

They persevered in the doing of these and many kinds of good works until the end. They died within a few days one of another. They were mourned with great weeping because of the odor of a good life which distinguished their days. They had spent their lives in the praise and the blessing of the Lord, and he bestowed many graces upon them, including the gift of sweet accord during the lifetime they had dedicated to his service. Nor were they separated in death: one died right after the other. They are remembered, and even to the present day their story is retold as are the lives of the saints, by people who knew them.

The plea of a young nobleman is rejected

All candidates were received personally by St. Francis — he perceives worldliness behind a young nobleman's display of pious emotion — the young man is quick to rejoin his family.

At the time when no-one was received into the Order of the Brothers without the consent of St. Francis, there came to him, along with some others wanting to enter the Order, the son of a nobleman — noble in the eyes of the world — of Lucca. St. Francis was very ill at the time and was staying in the palace of the bishop of Assisi.

When the brothers presented them to St. Francis, the nobleman's son bowed before him, and wept while begging to be received among the brothers of the Order. St. Francis, with his keen insight, understood with whom he was dealing. He said, "You wretched and fleshly minded man, you lie to the Holy Spirit and you lie to me. You shed tears, but it is the flesh and not the spirit they spring from."

No sooner had he said these things than the young nobleman's relatives arrived outside the palace on horseback. Hearing the clatter of the horses, he looked out the window and saw his relatives there. He got up and went out to them. He returned with them to the world, behaving as St. Francis, by the light of the Spirit, had known he would. The brothers and the others present marveled at this, and they glorified and praised God in his saint.

Proper food is brought to ailing St. Francis

The Saint has difficulty in eating — the rare foods he can eat are brought providentially.

At one time when he was gravely ill and dwelling in that same palace, the brothers coaxed him and tried to persuade him to eat. He told them, "I don't feel like eating. If though I had some fish, the kind called *squalus*, maybe I could eat."

145

He had hardly finished saying this when a man came carrying a basket. In it he had three large, nicely prepared *squalus* and a good quantity of shrimps. The holy Father ate them with pleasure. The basket of food had been sent by Brother Gerard, the Minister at Rieti.

At this manifestation of St. Francis's holiness the brothers were overcome with admiration. They praised the Lord who had satisfied his servant with things they could not have got for him. It was wintertime and in those parts things of the sort were not to be had.

St. Francis discerns the thoughts of a humiliated companion

Because of weakness and illness the Saint rides a donkey — the companion driving it is of distinguished family — St. Francis shows him consideration and deference on sensing his unspoken complaints.

At one time St. Francis was traveling with a brother, a spiritual man, who was the son of one of Assisi's great and powerful families. St. Francis, being weak and very ill, road on a donkey. The brother was wearied from traveling and began thinking to himself, "This man's family was not as highly stationed as mine, and here am I walking behind him, and driving his beast for him, all tired out." While these thoughts were passing through his mind, of a sudden St. Francis got down from the donkey. He said, "Brother, it is not right nor proper that I should ride while you walk on foot. In the world you were nobler and more powerful than I." The brother was at once astonished and ashamed. Weeping he threw himself at the holy Father's feet, confessed his thoughts and avowed his fault.

He marveled at St. Francis's great holiness because he had been so quick to know his thoughts. When the brothers requested the Lord Pope Gregory and the Cardinals at Assisi to canonize St. Francis, they made a report of this incident in testimonial.

St. Francis comes forth from seclusion to bless an unannounced Brother

In a lenten season the Saint observes the utmost seclusion — a brother comes for a blessing and in leaving is not disappointed.

There was a brother, a spiritual man and friend of God who lived in a place of the brothers at Rieti. One day he came devoutly to the hermitage to the brothers at Greccio where St. Francis was staying. He wanted to see him and get his blessing. When he arrived, St. Francis had already eaten and gone back to the cell where he prayed and slept. It was a lenten season when he would only leave his cell at mealtime, and then return to it immediately. Since the brother was obliged to go back to his place the same day, he was sad and disappointed at not finding St. Francis. He attributed the misfortune to his sins.

St. Francis's companions consoled him, and he took leave of them. He had started back to his own place, and had gone a stone's throw along the way when St. Francis, by the will of the Lord, came out of his cell and called to one of his companions who was accompanying the brother as far as the lake spring. He said to the companion, "Tell that brother to look at me." The brother turned his face to St. Francis who made a sign of the cross and blessed him. The brother rejoiced inwardly and outwardly, giving praise to the Lord who had fulfilled his desire. He was all the more consoled because it had been God's will that the holy Father should bless him without his asking it or having said a word about it.

The companions of St. Francis and the other brothers of the place marveled at what they considered to be a great miracle, because no-one had told St. Francis that the brother had come. Indeed, neither St. Francis's companions nor any other brother would presume to go to him without being called. Not only there, but wherever St. Francis went for a period of prayer, he wanted to stay in a place so secluded that nobody would go to him unless he were called.

A lesson on poverty and humility
on the feast of the Nativity

On the occasion of a Minister's visit the table for the
Nativity feast is prepared showily — St. Francis enacts
a scene to teach loyalty to our Lord's poverty and
humility.

At one time a Minister of the brothers came to see
St. Francis and stayed in the place where he was
to celebrate the feast of the Lord's Nativity with
him. The brothers of the place set the table elaborately
for the feast of the Nativity on the occasion of the Minister's visit, using fine white table cloths they had pur-
chased, and glass tumblers for drinking. In the midst
of these preparations, St. Francis came down from his
cell to eat. He saw that the table had been raised up high
from the floor and was set in fine style.

Taking care not to be seen, he got the hat of a poor
man who had come that day, and the staff he held in his
hand. In a hushed voice he signaled to one of his companions to come to him, and then went outside the door
of the hermitage without being noticed by the other
brothers of the house.

In the meantime the brothers came in and sat at
table, for it was the holy Father's custom to have them
start eating when they wished if he did not appear at
the usual time for the meal. His companion shut the door
and waited inside, close by it. St. Francis knocked on the
door and the brother opened it for him. St. Francis

149

entered with the hat hanging on his back and gripping the staff in his hand as a traveler does. Standing at the door of the house where the brothers were eating he assumed the meek posture of a poor beggar and called out, "For the love of the Lord God, give alms to this poor, sick traveler." The Minister and the other brothers saw right away who he was. The Minister answered, "Brother, we are poor men too. There are many of us and we need the alms we are eating, but for the love of that Lord you have called upon, come into the house, and we'll give you a part of the alms the Lord has given us."

When he had entered and stood before the brothers' table, the Minister handed him the bowl from which he was eating along with some bread. St. Francis took it and sat on the ground by the fire in front of the brothers who were sitting at the raised table. He sighed and said to the brothers, "When I saw the table set in such elegant, fine style, it did not look to me like the table for poor Religious who go begging from door to door every day. When we go begging and in all we do, we are obliged even more than other Religious to follow the example of humility and poverty which the Son of God left us. To this we have been called, and we have vowed before God and man to do it. I think that I'm now sitting the way a brother ought to sit."

At this the brothers felt ashamed for they recognized the truth of what St. Francis said. Some began to weep bitterly at the sight of him sitting on the ground and at the thought of the very holy and virtuous way he had found to correct them.

He also said that the brothers' tables ought to be humble and simple, so that seculars would be edified by them, and said too that if the brothers invited a poor man to eat, he should sit with them rather than down on the ground with the brothers sitting on higher seats.

The future Pope Gregory IX is given a practical lesson on gospel poverty

The Bishop of Ostia and his suite visit the Portiuncula — sleeping and eating conditions are described — the practical lesson moves the visitors to compunction.

Such was their mode of life when the Lord Pope Gregory, still Bishop of Ostia, came to the brothers' place at St. Mary of the Portiuncula. He entered the brothers' house and went to see their dormitory. Many knights, monks and other clerics were in his company. When he saw that the brothers slept on the ground with nothing under them but a little straw, with no pillow, and with miserable covers that were practically worn to shreds, he began to weep and shed tears before them all.

He said, "Look, here is where the brothers sleep! Surely we are wretched men for we use superfluous things no matter what we do. What is to become of us ?" He and the others had been greatly edified by what they had seen.

He saw no table in the house because the brothers ate on the ground. From the beginning, when the place was first built, the brothers of the place ate on the ground whether they were few or many. Indeed their place was more frequented than any other. For a long time brothers of the whole Order would come there, and all the men intending to enter the Order were accepted there. As long as the holy Father lived, the brothers of the place sat on the ground to eat according to his example and will.

St. Francis is pleased with the place and the people at Greccio

The Saint preferred Greccio because of the poverty — through example and preaching people were converted to devout gospel life — disasters and penance — return of prosperity — relapse to evil ways and punishment as St. Francis had prophesied.

St. Francis liked the place of the brothers at Greccio because it was austere and poor, and the people of the village, although they were very poor and simple pleased him more than any others of that country. The holy Father often went there to rest and stay a while, especially since there was a very poor little cell, secluded and at a distance, where he could stay.

152

By his own example and preaching, and by his brothers' as well, many men of the locality entered the Order. Many women preserved their virginity. They wore religious habits while continuing to live in their homes. They would live the common life in a holy manner, chastise their bodies with fasting, and they prayed. In the eyes of the laymen and of the brothers they did not seem like persons living in the midst of worldly doings, and living with their families. Rather they had the air of women who ordinarily live among holy persons and Religious. They behaved as if they had been in the Lord's service for a long time, whereas they were actually young and very simple girls. Indeed, when St. Francis was with his brothers he would often speak joyfully of the men and women of the village saying, "You won't find as many people converted to penitence in any large city as you do in Greccio, and it's only a tiny village!"

When the brothers of the place would praise the Lord in the evening, as was their custom in many places at that time, the villagers, adults and little children, would come out and stand on the road that passed alongside the village, and would cry out, "May the Lord God be praised!" Even babies not yet able to talk would praise the Lord as they could while watching what the brothers did.

In those times the people of the village were suffering disasters that had beset them for a number of years. Big wolves were eating men, and hail was ruining their fields and vineyards year after year. Wherefore St. Francis said while preaching to them one day, "I have an announcement to make to you in God's honor and praise. If each one of you will correct his sinful ways and convert to God with a whole heart, and with the will and intention of persevering, I can trust the Lord Jesus Christ to be merciful to you. He will free you right now from the scourge of wolves and hailstorms you have had to endure for so long, and make you abound in both spiritual and temporal goods. ''

'' But I also announce to you — may it not come to pass — if later you return to your vomit, these plagues and pestilences will come upon you again with greater disasters added to them. ''

It came to pass, by divine dispensation and the holy Father's merits, that from that very hour the disasters ceased. This was beyond all doubt a great miracle because the hail would fall on neighboring fields and destroy them without touching the fields of these villagers even though they were right next to them. The people prospered and abounded in spiritual and temporal goods for sixteen to twenty years. After that they became proud of their prosperity and vented their hatred one upon another. They struck down and killed their fellowmen with the sword, secretly killed beasts belonging to others, plundered and robbed by night, and committed many other crimes.

When the Lord saw that their works were evil and they were not observing what he had proclaimed to them through his servant, his anger was enkindled, and he withdrew the hand of his mercy from them. The scourge of hailstorms and wolves recommenced as the holy Father had foretold, and worse disasters than before befell them. The entire village was burned down. The people lost all they had and could escape only with their lives.

The brothers and other people who had heard what the holy Father had said in his predictions of prosperity and adversity marveled at his holiness, for they saw everything fulfilled to the letter.

St. Francis preaches peace to the Perugians

Knights wilfully interrupt the sermon of Francis the Assisan — he admonishes a return to penance, fear of God, and peace, and warns of punishment — the haughty Perugians punish themselves — St. Francis knew how to correct sinners effectively.

At one time St. Francis was at Perugia preaching in the city square to a great crowd of people gathered there to hear him. His sermon was brought to a halt by some Perugian knights who came galloping about the square for the sport of it with their swords drawn. The men and women intent upon hearing St. Francis preach rebuked them, but the knights paid no attention.

St. Francis faced the knights, and in a transport of the spirit cried out, "Listen to what I say, and heed what the Lord proclaims to you through me, his servant. Mind that you do not say, 'Don't listen to him — he is an Assisan!'" St. Francis said this because the usual hatred between Assisans and Perugians was rife. He also told them, "The Lord has exalted you and made you a grander people than those in your neighboring cities. For this you should give your Creator all the greater recognition. What you should do is not only to humble yourselves all the more before almighty God, but before your neighbors too. Instead you have become haughty of heart and arrogant; you have become proud because you're strong; you've taken to plundering the people in the neighboring towns and you've killed a lot of them. Therefore, I say to you, unless you convert quickly to him, and make satisfaction for the wrongs you've done to those other cities, the Lord, who leaves no wrong pass without due chastisement, will punish you, disgrace you, and be avenged. He will so stir you up to fighting that you will fight one against the other. You will suffer far more terribly from the havoc of uprisings and internal warfare than you could have from anything the people in the other cities would ever have been able to do to you."

Indeed the vices of the Perugians were a flagrant offence to God and neighbor and St. Francis did not pass them over in silence when he preached. He had been given such abundant grace by God that everybody who saw or heard him, common folk or persons of consequence, held him in fear and veneration. When St. Francis admonished a man, he might feel ashamed, but he would not fail to be edified. On some occasions he would pray with particular ardor for such a person, who would be straightway converted to the Lord.

It came about through divine permission that just a few days later strife broke out between the knights and the people. The people drove the knights out of the city. The knights with the Church's support, ravaged the fields, vineyards, and trees belonging to the people. Whatever damage they could do, that they did. The people on their part ravaged the fields, vineyards and trees of the knights' property.

Thus the Perugians were chastised by a greater punishment than all the peoples they had wronged could have done to them, and St. Francis's prediction was fulfilled to the letter.

In answer to the Saint's prayer an abbot receives a grace

In holy conversation with an abbot St. Francis promises a prayer — when the Saint prays the abbot experiences a rapture.

While St. Francis was traveling through a certain region, the abbot of a monastery came out to meet him. This abbot held him in veneration and loved him. The abbot descended from his horse and talked with the Saint for some hours about the salvation of his soul.

When they were taking leave of each other, the abbot devoutly made a request of St. Francis, asking him to pray to the Lord for his soul. St. Francis told him, "I shall do so gladly." After the abbot had left him and gone a short distance along his way, St. Francis said to his companion, "Brother, let us stop here a while. I want to pray for that abbot as I promised him." He then prayed for him.

This was according to his custom. When anyone devoutly asked St. Francis to pray to God for his soul, he would pray for that person as soon as he could lest later on he forget about it.

The abbot was still traveling along the road, and had not gone far when the Lord suddenly visited his heart. A sweet warmth enveloped his face, and his spirit was born aloft to the heights, but for only a brief moment. Upon returning to his senses he realized that St. Francis had prayed for him. Thereupon he praised God, and inwardly and outwardly rejoiced.

Because of this evidence of the holy Father's exceedingly great sanctity, the abbot thereafter held St. Francis in still greater devotion. He himself was convinced as long as he lived that this was a great miracle, and he often recounted to the brothers and other people what he had experienced.

St. Francis's keen sympathy
for the suffering Jesus Christ

St. Francis's ailments are specified — the eye disease
was contracted in Egypt — because of sorrow for Our
Lord's sufferings he has no thought for his own — an
instance of weeping for the suffering Lord at the Portiuncula — he has no need of consolation from Scripture
reading because of the vividness of his meditations —
he refuses bodily care for his eye disease and other
ailments.

For a long time St. Francis had had ailments of
the liver, the spleen, and the stomach, and he
had these ailments until he died. Another ailment
was a grave disease of the eyes. He had had it since the
time he had gone overseas and preached to the Sultan
of Babylon and Egypt. He had contracted the disease
as a result of his strenuous and exhausting journey when,
both going and coming, he had had to bear extreme
heat. He would not concern himself with cures for any
of these ailments even though the brothers and other
persons, in their compassion and pity for him, tried to
persuade him to have them taken care of.

It was because of the spiritual ardor inspiring him
since he was first converted to Christ that he had no
mind for medical care. Daily he derived such great
sweetness and compassion from the humility and the words
and deeds of the Son of God that anything bitter for the
flesh was accepted by him as sweetness and was sweet
for him. Each day he sorrowed so profoundly and was

159

so keenly afflicted, inwardly and outwardly, by the sufferings and sorrows Christ bore for our sake that he gave no heed to his own sufferings.

For instance, one day a few years after his conversion, he was walking along the road not far from the church of St. Mary of the Portiuncula, weeping and wailing in a loud voice as he went along. A man, who was a very spiritual person, saw him there and spoke to him. We have known the man and have learned of this incident from him. He had treated St. Francis with gentle kindness and had encouraged him before he had any brothers, and he continued to do so afterwards.

The man thought St. Francis was in pain because of some illness, and pityingly asked him, "Brother, what's the matter?" He answered, "I ought to travel everywhere, and not be ashamed, weeping and wailing for the passion of my Lord." The man then walked along with him, he too weeping and shedding abundant tears.

On another occasion, during the time of his eye disease that was very painful for him, a Minister said to him, "Brother, why not have your companion read to you from the prophets, or from some other part of the Scriptures? Your spirit would exult on hearing the sacred reading and you would get some consolation from it." He knew how St. Francis rejoiced in the Lord upon hearing the divine Scriptures read. But St. Francis replied, "Brother, every day I find so much sweetness and consolation in my memory from meditating upon the examples left by the Son of God that if I should live until the end of the world there would be little need of my hearing or meditating upon any more Scripture reading."

Often he would call to mind and tell the brothers these words of David: "My soul refuses comfort (*Ps* 77, 2b)." He felt obliged, as he often repeated to the brothers, to be the model and example for all the brothers. Hence he would refuse not only medicines, but even necessary food during his illnesses. Moreover, keeping these things in mind, he would always treat his body with austerity, whether in appearance he was well — for actually he was always weak and ailing — or whether he was afflicted with his illnesses.

The Saint's absolute candor in fulfilling his duty of being an example

A dramatic declaration of self indulgence arouses the people's compunction — the Saint wants hidden acts to be known by men as they are by God — he opposes hypocrisy — a fur lining must be made evident on the outside of a garment — he immediately avows a feeling of vainglory.

At one time when he had somewhat recovered from an extremely serious illness, he reflected on what he had eaten while he was sick and called to mind that he had sometimes eaten servings of good food. Actually he had eaten very little for the very reason that he was unable to eat much food during the

161

many and various illnesses he had been suffering over a lengthy period. However, on a day when he was not yet entirely cured of a quartan fever, he had the people of Assisi summoned to the main square to hear a sermon. When he had finished preaching, he told the people not to leave until he had returned. Then he went into the church of St. Rufinus and down into the chamber known as the confession. With him were brother Peter Cattanii whom he had appointed the first Minister General, and some brothers.

He gave instructions to Brother Peter with the admonition that he must obey him, make no objections, and say and do in his regard whatever he asked. Brother Peter answered, "Brother, I cannot, neither should I will anything except what your good pleasure might be in whatever concerns me or you." St. Francis then took off his tunic and told Brother Peter to lead him by a rope tied around his neck out before the people. He told another brother to take a bowl of ashes, go up to the place where he had been preaching, and when they had arrived, pour ashes on his head and rub them in. This brother was too overcome by his feelings of pity and compassion to comply and failed to obey. But Brother Peter went out and led him along as he had been ordered. He was weeping, as were the other brothers.

When the holy Father came back in this state, naked, to the place where he had been preaching, he faced the people and said, "You believe I am a holy man. There are other men who have followed my example by leaving the world, entering the Order of the brothers and living

162

their life. But I confess to God and to you that while I was sick I ate meat and took meat broth."

Thereupon practically everybody began to weep out of pity and compassion for him, and with all the more reason since it was wintertime, the weather was cold, and he had not yet fully recovered from his quartan fever.

They beat their breasts and accused themselves saying, "We know what sort of life this saint has led. He has practiced abstinence and austerity, and he has been harshly severe with his body ever since he was converted to Christ. We see him here alive, but his flesh is in such a state that he looks as if he were dead ahead of time. He accuses himself, and shames his body because he only allowed himself what was reasonable and clearly needed for his health. What then are we to do, wretched creatures that we are? All our life long we have lived and wanted to live according to the will and desires of our flesh."

A similar incident occurred during a St. Martin's lent he was passing at a certain hermitage when the brothers had used lard in preparing some food for him. They did this because olive oil was not good for his health when he was ill. When his lent was ended he preached a sermon to a large congregation of people who had gathered not far from the hermitage.

At the beginning of the sermon he said, "You have come here to me very devoutly with the idea that I am a holy man. But I confess to God and to you that during this lent, in this hermitage, I have eaten food cooked with lard."

. There were times when he would eat with his brothers or with friends of his brothers, and he would be served a plate of good food because his ailing body was evidently in need of it. Rarely if ever would he fail, while still in the house or on leaving it, to declare frankly to the brothers and to layfolk who knew nothing about it, "I have eaten such and such food," for he did not want to leave hidden before men anything that was seen by God.

Wherever he might be, and before any Religious or layman whatsoever, if ever he felt he had been stirred by vainglory, pride, or any vice, he would straightway confess it to them baldly and without dissimulation. In this regard he told his companions one day, "When I am in the hermitage and the other places where I stay, I want to live before God just as men know and see me. If they believe I am a holy man and I am not really leading a life befitting a holy man, I would be a hypocrite."

Once in wintertime one of his companions, the one who was his Guardian, thought he should do something for his ailing spleen and the coldness of his stomach. He got a fox hide and asked the holy Father to let him sew it on the under side of his tunic against his spleen and stomach as protection against the great cold. He was aware that from the time St. Francis began to serve Christ until the day of his death he would never wear nor have more than one tunic, and this had to be patched for he insisted on wearing a habit that was patched.

St. Francis told him, "If you want me to have that fur on the inside of my tunic, then have another piece of it sewn on the outside too so as to give the people some sign that I have fur on the inside. " He had it done that way, but he rarely made use of it even though his illnesses made it necessary.

Another time he was passing through the city of Assisi surrounded by a crowd of people. Among them was a poor little old woman who begged alms of him for the love of God. Without a moment's hesitation he gave her the cloak he was wearing. No sooner had he done this than he confessed before all the people that this gesture had aroused his vainglory.

We who were with him have seen and heard of many such examples. We cannot write about them all because such an account would be too long to narrate. However, St. Francis did take most exacting and very particular care not to be a hypocrite before God. Even though his body might be in need of a plate of good food because of his illness, he would firmly hold to his belief that he must present a good example to the brothers and other people, so as to obviate any occasion for complaint or giving bad example. He preferred to endure bodily trials, as he did endure them, to the day of his death, rather than fulfill his needs, even when he could well have done so before God and not fail in the giving of good example.

The composition of the Canticle of Brother Sun
at St. Damien's

St. Francis under obedience must have his eyes cured
— he stays more than fifty days at San Damiano —
unable to bear light on his eyes he is kept in a darkened
cell within the house — pain and tormenting mice
impede sleep — he implores consolation — the Lord
promises the treasure of the Kingdom of God in recompense for sufferings — he should be joyful in suffering — we should praise the lord and thank him in
gratitude for creatures without which we cannot live —
he specifies intentions and purposes and then composes
the *Canticle* — he composes music for singing it and
teaches it to some brothers.

The Bishop of Ostia, who was later to become
pope, was aware of how severe St. Francis then
was and constantly had been in the austere
treatment of his body. He saw that he had already begun
to lose his eyesight and would even so not let himself
be cured. With great sympathy and compassion he admonished him saying, " Brother, you refuse to get any help
for your eye disease. I don't think this is a good thing.
Your health and your life are extremely useful to you
and others. Now when your brothers are ill, you treat
them considerately. If you are merciful in caring for them,
then when you yourself are gravely ill, as quite clearly
you are now, you should not be cruel to yourself. I
therefore command you to get medical care. "

Two years before his death when he had already
become seriously ill, and was suffering particularly from

166

his diseased eyes, he was staying at St. Damien's in a cell made of matting. The Minister General saw how grievous his eye disease was and thought over the matter. He likewise commanded the holy Father to have himself cared for and given treatment. He even said that he wanted to be present when the doctor should undertake the cure, so as to make sure that he would be given the best possible medical care. He was wanting to give him some comfort, for he was suffering most painfully.

Meanwhile the weather was very cold and not the time for a cure.

For more than fifty days St. Francis lay there unable to bear either the light of day or the firelight at night. He stayed the whole time in the house, inside his little cell where it was dark. Moreover, his eyes gave him such atrocious pain, day and night, that it was not possible for him to get any rest or sleep at night. This was extremely bad for his eyes as it was for all the other ailments.

To make it still worse, there were mice to pester him if he tried to rest or sleep. There were many of them in that house and in that little cell where he lay, a cell made of matting and built up against the wall of the house. They ran over him and all around him; they kept him from sleeping; and they distracted him at prayer time. They tormented him not only at night, but during the day when they would climb up on his table while he was eating. His companions and he too believed this was a diabolical temptation, as indeed it was.

One night St. Francis's thoughts turned to the many grievous tribulations he had to bear, and he began pitying

167

himself. He said within himself, "O Lord, come to my aid, comfort me so that I can bear my illnesses with patience!"

Immediately it was said to him in spirit: "Tell me, Brother: Suppose someone were to give you a recompense for these illnesses and tribulations of yours. It would be a treasure so great and precious that if all the earth were pure gold, all the stones precious stones, and all the water balm, you would even so look upon all these materials as nothing, and esteem them as worth no more than mere earth, stones, and water in comparison with the great and precious treasure being given you. Wouldn't that make you happy?"

St. Francis replied, "Lord, a treasure like that would be a grand one, well worth striving for, extremely precious and much to be cherished and desired."

The One speaking told him, "Therefore, brother, rejoice and be thoroughly jubilant in your illnesses and tribulations, because you can be as sure of having it as if you were already in my Kingdom."

When he awoke in the morning, St. Francis said to his companions, "If an emperor were to give an entire kingdom to one of his servants, wouldn't that make the man happy? And if the emperor were to give him his whole empire, wouldn't that make him far happier?" Then he told them, "From now on I ought to be very joyful in my illnesses and tribulations, find my comfort in the Lord, and at all times give thanks to God the Father and his only Son, our Lord Jesus Christ, and the Holy Spirit for the immense grace and blessing given me. In his mercy he has deigned to give me, his unworthy servant, while I am still alive in my flesh, the assurance that I am going to receive the Kingdom.

"Therefore, to praise him, to console myself, and to edify my fellowmen, I'm going to compose a new *Praise of the Lord for his Creatures*. We use those creatures every day, and we can't live without them, and yet mankind uses them to offend their Creator. Not only that, but we are ungrateful for so many graces because we do not praise as we ought our Creator and giver of all good things."

Then he sat down, began to think, and after a while said:

All-highest, almighty good Lord,
to you be praise, glory and honor
and every blessing;
to you alone they are due,
and no man is worthy to speak your name.

Be praised, my Lord, in all your creatures,
especially for sire Brother Sun
who makes daytime,
and through him you give us light,
and he is beautiful, radiant with great splendor,
and he is a sign
that tells, All-highest, of you.

Be praised, my Lord, for Sister Moon and the stars;
you formed them in the sky,
bright and precious and beautiful.

Be praised, my Lord, for Brother Wind,
and for the air and the clouds,
and for fair, and every kind of weather,
by which you give your creatures food.

Be praised, my Lord, for Sister Water,
who is most useful and humble
and lovely and chaste.

Be praised, my Lord, for Brother Fire,
through whom you light up the night for us;
and he is beautiful and jolly
and lusty and strong.

Be praised, my Lord, for our Sister Mother Earth,
who keeps us, and feeds us,
and brings forth fruits of many kinds,
with colored flowers and plants as well.

Bless and praise my Lord,
thank him, and serve him
in all humility.

He then composed a melody for the verses so that
they could be sung, and taught his companions to sing
them.

St. Francis explains the use to be made of his Canticle

St. Francis teaches Pacificus and other brothers the pastoral use of the *Canticle* — the people are to be called to penitence — as minstrels of the Lord they should rouse souls to spiritual joy — he gives a name to the *Canticle* — Brother Sun in the morning and Brother Fire in the evening invite men to praise God — the Saint's pains are forgot in joyous praise through the singing of the *Canticle*.

In the great sweetness and consolation his spirit was enjoying he called for Brother Pacificus, the brother whom people had called the King of Verses when he was in the world, for he had been an accomplished master-singer in the courts. He assigned some good, spiritual brothers to him, who were to go about the country with him preaching and praising God. He intended, as he told them, that one of them who was a good preacher should first preach to the people, and when the sermon was done, they should all join in the singing of the *Praises of the Lord*, like the Lord's minstrels. When they had finished singing the *Praises*, the preacher should say to the people, "We are the Lord's minstrels, and we want to be paid for our performance. You can pay us by living in true penitence."

Then he remarked, "After all, what are servants of God if not, in a certain sense, his minstrels because we ought to rouse men's hearts and lift them to spiritual joy?" In saying this, he referred particularly to the Lesser

Brothers whom the Lord has given to the people for their salvation.

He gave a name to the *Praises of the Lord* he had composed, that is, to the canticle beginning with the words: *All-highest, almighty good Lord.* He called them the *Canticle of Brother Sun,* for the reason that the sun is more beautiful than all other creatures, and has a greater resemblance to God. He explained, "When the sun comes up in the morning, everybody should praise God, his Creator, because he gives us light for our eyes in daytime. Then, when evening comes and it gets dark, everybody should praise God for another creature, Brother Fire, because he gives us light for our eyes at nighttime." He went on to say, "We are all like blind men, and the Lord provides us with these two creatures so that we can have light for our eyes to see."

Whether in good or bad health, he was always ready and willing to praise the Lord, and with zeal he called upon everybody else to do the same thing. When he felt weighed down by sickness, he would intone the *Praises of the Lord* and then have his companions sing them so that his thoughts would be drawn to the Lord's praise and the painful torments of his ailments would be forgot. This was his practice until he died.

St. Francis composes a stanza on pardon
for his Canticle

To reconcile the mayor and the bishop he has the
Canticle with a newly composed stanza sung before them
and their company.

During that same time when St. Francis lay ill
and had already composed the *Praises*, the bishop
then incumbent of Assisi excommunicated the
mayor of Assisi then in office. The mayor, enangered
against him, had it loudly and well proclaimed throughout
the city of Assisi that no-one should sell to, buy from,
or enter into any contract with the bishop. And so the
two remained intensely hating each other.

St. Francis, extremely ill as he was, felt pity for them.
He was especially grieved because no Religious or layman
had tried to intervene and bring them to peace and accord. He said to his companions, " This is a shameful
thing for us servants of God. The bishop and the mayor
are hating each other and no-one will intervene to bring
them to peace and accord. " So on that occasion he
composed the following stanza to be added to his *Praises:*

Be praised, my Lord, for those who grant pardon
for love of you
and bear with sickness and tribulation.
Blessed are those who bear these things peaceably
Because, All-highest,
they will be granted a crown by you.

173

When he had finished it, he called one of his companions and told him, "Go and ask the mayor on my behalf to come to the bishop's palace with the notables of the city and anyone else he might bring with him."

When that brother had gone, he told two other companions, "Go and sing the *Canticle of Brother Sun* before the bishop and the mayor and the men in attendance. I am trusting in the Lord to humble their hearts and they will make peace with each other and be friends and love each other as before."

When all these persons were assembled in the courtyard of the bishop's palace, the two brothers stepped forward. One of them said, "St. Francis, who is now ill, has composed *Praises of the Lord for his Creatures* in praise of him and for the edification of his fellowmen. He requests you to listen to them with great devotion." They then began singing the verses. The mayor at once stood up, and with joined hands listened devoutly as if to the Lord's Gospel, even weeping. When the singing of the *Praises of the Lord* came to an end, the mayor declared before them all, "Surely I would forgive the Lord Bishop; I ought to regard him as my lord. And even if anyone killed my brother or my son, I would forgive him too!" Then he threw himself at the Lord Bishop's feet and declared, "See, I am prepared to make amends to you for everything, in whatever way it may be your pleasure to have it done, for love of the Lord Jesus Christ and his servant St. Francis."

The bishop arose, lifted the mayor with his hands, and said to him, "Because of my office it behooves me to be humble, but by nature my wrath is easily aroused. You must forgive me." They then embraced each other with kindness and affection, and kissed each other.

The brothers marveled greatly at this evidence of St. Francis's holiness because what he had foretold about their coming to peaceful accord was verified to the letter. All the others who had assisted at the event and had heard what was said believed it to be a great miracle. They attributed to the merits of St. Francis the Lord's speedy visitation of these two men who with no further remembrance of such clamorous strife returned to such grand accord.

Therefore, we who were with St. Francis testify that whenever he would predict, "Something is so or will be so," it would become so practically to the letter, and we have seen so many such things with our eyes that writing a narration of it all would take a long time.

St. Francis sends a message to be sung to the Poor Clares

During his stay at St. Damien's he had not been able to see the nuns — he has his companions take them a message and sing a newly composed song for them — a summary report of the message's contents.

In those days and in that same place, after St. Francis had composed the *Praises of the Lord for the Creatures*, he also composed a holy message with music. He wanted to give the Poor Ladies of the St. Damien monastery some consolation, for he knew they were not a little anguished because of his own illness.

Since his illnesses did not permit him to go to visit and console them personally, he wanted his companions to announce his message. With these words he intended to make a clear, brief declaration of his will, for that time and all time, in their regard, telling them how they should be of one mind and deal one with another in charity. It was through his example and teaching, at the time when there were still few brothers that they had been converted to Christ. Their conversion and mode of life had not only inspired and edified the Order of the brothers, whose little plant they were, but as well the universal Church.

St. Francis well knew that from the beginning of their conversion they had lived, as they still lived, a rigorous and very poor life, both because they willed it and because necessity obliged it. For this reason his pious sentiments always went out to them. Wherefore in this message he called upon them to be faithful in observing, both in life and death, holy charity, holy poverty, and holy obedience, for indeed the Lord had called them into one from many parts for this purpose. Especially he exhorted them to be prudent in providing for bodily needs from the alms the Lord would give them, and do so in joy and thanksgiving. Also, the sisters who were well should always be patient in their painstaking care of their ailing sisters, and the ailing Sisters should remain patient in their illnesses and trials.

St. Francis goes to Fonte Colombo for eye treatment

He travels on horseback with eyes covered because of illness — description of treatment — Brother Elias does not come as expected — the Saint delays treatment because he wants care of his person only under orders from another — the brothers are assured a reward from the Lord for fatiguing services to him.

When the suitable time for the cure of his eye disease was approaching, St. Francis left that place. Because of his severely diseased eyes, he wore a large hood the brothers had made for him over his head. To this was sewn a piece of cloth made of wool and linen to cover his eyes, for the pain caused by his eye disease was so great he could not stand seeing daylight. His companions led him on horseback to the hermitage of Fonte Colombo near Rieti for consultation with a doctor of that city who understood the cure of eye diseases.

When the doctor came there he told St. Francis he would have to cauterize him from his jaw to the eyebrow above that eye which was more diseased than the other. However, St. Francis did not want to begin the cure before Brother Elias came. They waited for him, but he was impeded by his many affairs and did not arrive. St. Francis was still hesitant about having the cure begun.

Finally when it became absolutely necessary, and especially since obedience to the Lord Bishop of Ostia and the Minister General obliged him, he decided to do as he had been commanded. It was for him a grave matter to have so much attention given to his person, and it was for this reason that he had been wanting the Minister to decide on whatever action was to be taken.

Afterwards, on a night when the pains of his illness kept him from getting any sleep, and he was feeling sorrowful for his pitiable state, he said to his companions, "Don't let all the work you're doing in looking after my illnesses be burdensome to you and damp your spirits, because the Lord is going to reward you on my behalf. He will remit you in this world and in the next the profits from the activities you weren't able to carry out because you had to tend my illnesses. You will gain greater profit from what you're doing than those who are promoting the good of the whole Order and life of the brothers. You may even say to me, 'We're spending from our pockets on you, and the Lord will be our debtor in your stead.'"

In saying this the holy Father had in mind giving them some encouragement and rousing their wearied and weakened spirits. He was afraid their strenuous labors would be an occasion of temptation. They could say, "We aren't able to pray and we can't stand so much work either," and if they were to become sluggish and faint-hearted, they could lose the fruit of their labors.

Brother Fire is gentle during the cautery

St. Francis expresses his affection for Brother Fire — he
reprimands the brothers for weakness — he has been
spared the natural pain of the hot iron — a report on
the unsuccessful treatment.

One day the doctor came bringing with him the
iron he used for cauterizing eye diseases. He had
a fire made to heat the iron, and when the fire
was burning, he put the iron into it. To comfort his
spirit, and so as to keep from being frightened, St. Francis
said to the fire, "O Fire, brother mine, noble and useful
above all creatures the All-highest has created, be kind
to me in this hour. In the past I have loved you, and still
love you for love of the Lord who created you. I pray
our Creator who created you that he temper your heat
enough for me to bear it." At the end of his prayer he
made a sign of the cross over the fire.

But all of us who were with him felt such pity and
compassion that we fled and left him with no-one but the
doctor. When the cautery was done, we came back to
him. He told us, "Oh you weak and of little faith, why
did you flee? I tell you truly that I felt no pain at all
and I didn't even feel the heat of the fire. So if the cautery
hasn't been done well, let him go ahead and do it better."

The doctor marveled greatly at this, believing it a
great miracle, because the holy Father had hardly stirred.
He said, "My brothers, you may be sure I was afraid
this weak and ailing man wouldn't be able to stand such

179

a severe cautery as this. I would be afraid that even a strong man, sound in body, wouldn't be able to stand it, and I have had experience in such matters. "

The cauterized area, extending from his ear to his eyebrow, was long, due to the copious pus that had been flowing into his eyes daily, both day and night, for many years. In the doctor's opinion the veins between the ear and eyebrow had to be destroyed. However, other physicians were of the opinion that all this was bad for him. They were right, because it did him no good at all. Another doctor perforated both his ears, and this did him no good either.

St. Francis's regard for fire and other creatures

The Saint delighted in creatures and suffered on seeing them mistreated — he has the day's Gospel read when without Mass at La Verna — various incidents illustrate his affectionate regard for creatures — flowers and other creatures summon us to the praise of God — the *Canticle* testifies to his joy in creatures and is intended to arouse all men's praise of God.

It should be no matter for surprise if fire and other creatures would sometimes venerate St. Francis. We who were with him have seen with what warm affection he loved them, how he revered them, and what great delight he took in them. We have seen too how badly he felt about it if he saw anyone mistreating them. He talked to them with inward and outward joy as if with creatures who knew, understood and talked about God. On such occasions he would often be rapt into contemplation of God.

At one time he was sitting beside the fire when, without his noticing it, the linen clothing on his leg caught fire. He soon felt the heat of the fire and his companion saw that the fire was burning his clothes. The brother ran to put out the flame, but the holy Father told him, " My very dear brother, don't hurt Brother Fire!" and absolutely refused to let him extinguish it. The brother rushed to find the brother who was his Guardian and brought him in. So, against St. Francis's wishes the brother put out the fire.

He did not want candles, lamps or fires to be put out as is ordinarily done when they are no longer needed, so great was his affectionate regard for fire. Nor would he let the brother throw burning or smoking wood outside, as is commonly done, but had it spread carefully on the ground out of reverence for the One of whom the fire is a creature.

Once when St. Francis was making a forty-day retreat on Mount Alverna, his companion lit a fire at mealtime in the cell where he ate. He left the fire burning and went to find St. Francis in the cell where he prayed and slept according to his custom, and there read him the Holy Gospel of the day's Mass. When St. Francis could not assist at Mass, he always wanted to hear the Gospel of the day read before eating.

When St. Francis came to eat in the cell where the

fire was lit, the flames were already leaping to the roof of the cell and had set it on fire. His companion began extinguishing the fire as well as he could but it was too much for him to do by himself. St. Francis would not help him. Instead, he took a hide which he used as a cover at night and went into the forest.

The brothers dwelling there lived at a distance from the cell because it was located far from their place. When they discovered that the cell was burning, they came and put out the fire.

Afterwards St. Francis came back to eat. When the meal was done he told his companion, "I won't have this hide over me any more because I was selfish and wouldn't let Brother Fire eat it."

Likewise when he washed his hands he would choose a place where the water would not be walked upon afterwards. When he had to walk over stones, he would go with fear and reverence because of love of Him who is called *the Rock*. Thus if he were to recite the psalm verse, "You have lifted me up upon the rock (*Ps* 61,3)," he would reverently and devoutly say, "You have lifted me to beneath the feet of the Rock."

He told the brother who cut firewood not to chop down whole trees, but to cut only a part of a tree so as to leave a part standing. He gave this order to a certain brother at a place he was staying.

He told the brother who took care of the garden not to plant the whole space with edible plants only. A part of the ground should be reserved for growing ornamental plants which in their season would bloom with Brother

Flowers. He said that the brother gardener should plant a pretty little flower bed somewhere in the plot with various kinds of sweetly scented herbs and flowering plants. These would in their season invite all who saw them to praise God, for every creature says and cries out, "God made me for you, oh man!"

We who were with him have seen him inwardly and outwardly rejoice in almost every kind of creature. He took such pleasure in touching them and looking at them that his spirit seemed to be in heaven rather than on earth. This is quite clearly and truly the case because it was on account of the many consolations he had always had in God's creatures that not long before his death he composed the *Praises of the Lord for His Creatures*, so that the hearts of the people hearing them would be roused to the praise of God, and God would be praised in his creatures by everybody.

St. Francis aids a needy woman

St. Francis contrives a plan to help a woman needier than himself and relieves his wealthy doctor of a financial burden — the traits of a woman hardened to a wretched life are realistically described.

At that same time a very poor woman from Machilone came to Rieti to have her eye disease treated. One day when the doctor had come to see St. Francis, he told him, "Brother, a woman with diseased eyes has come to me and she is so poor I have to give her my service for the love of God and pay for her keep as well." On hearing this St. Francis was moved by pity for her. He called one of his companions, the one who was his Guardian, and said, "Brother Guardian, we must give back goods that belong to someone else." The Guardian answered, "What do we have to give back, brother?" St. Francis said, "This cape. We got it on loan from that poor woman with the eye disease, and we have to give it back." His Guardian said, "Do what you think best."

St. Francis then joyfully called a certain spiritual man whom he knew and told him, "Take this cape and twelve loaves of bread with it. Then go to a poor and ailing woman the doctor is treating, and tell her what I'll tell you to say. He'll show you which one she is. Tell her, 'The poor man you loaned this cape to thanks you for the loan of it. Take what is yours.'"

The man then went and told the woman what St. Francis had told him to say. She though did not recognize it as anything belonging to her and she answered in fear and shame, "Let me alone; I don't know what you're talking about!" He then put the cape and the twelve loaves of bread into her hands. This convinced her he was speaking in earnest. She took the things, still afraid, but with joy throbbing in her heart. That night she became anxious, fearing someone would come and take the things away from her. She got up in secret and went back to her own home with them delighted.

St. Francis had also told his Guardian he should pay her daily expenses for the love of God.

Some examples of zealous poverty and joyful charity

The Saint readily deprives himself of essential needs — he insists upon charity in observing obedience — his own and the brothers' hardships consequent upon his giving away his clothes — he had more than one tunic only on the occasion of a troublesome illness — he rode instead of walking only when physically disabled — a brother's joy in giving away his cape is a sign of a grace — a valuable gospel book is better given in alms to " Mother " than read.

We therefore who were with St. Francis give testimony about him, and declare that whether he was in good or bad health, his charity and pity were so great toward his brothers, as well as to any poor people, whether they were healthy or sick, that he would give away things he needed for his own body. Sometimes they were things the brothers, in their devotion to him, had acquired with considerable trouble. First he would win over our sentiments with gentle words so that we would not be too upset, and then in a very joyful spirit deprive himself of things he needed badly for his own body so as to give them to others.

On this account, the Minister General and his Guardian commanded him not to give his tunic to any brother without their permission. It would happen at times that brothers, out of devotion for him, would ask him for his tunic and he would give it to them immediately. Or if he should see a brother very ill or clothed badly he was likely to give him his tunic, at times dividing it, giving

185

a part to the other and keeping a part for himself, for he refused to have or to wear more than one tunic.

At one time when he was traveling through a certain country to preach, it happened that two French brothers met him and received great spiritual encouragement from their conversation with him. On taking leave they asked him, in their devotion, to give them his tunic for the love of God. He had no sooner heard "for the love of God" than he took off his tunic and remained naked for some hours. One of the brothers took off his tunic and gave it to him.

It was St. Francis's custom that whenever anyone said to him, "For the love of God give me your tunic, or your cord," or whatever he might have, immediately he would give it to the person out of reverence for the Lord who is named *Love* (cf. *I Jn* 4,16). In fact it was very displeasing to him, and often he rebuked the brothers for it, if he heard them use the words *love of God* for trivial motives. He would say, "The love of God is so extremely exalted that it should only be mentioned rarely, when one is in extreme need, and then with great reverence."

He often endured severe trials and tribulations when he gave his tunic or a part of it to someone. He could not easily find another or have another made right away because he always wanted to have and wear a wretchedly poor tunic made out of odd pieces, and sometimes he wanted it patched inside and out. Rarely if ever would he have or wear a tunic made from new cloth. He would get a tunic one of the brothers had worn a long time.

186

Sometimes he would get a part of a tunic from one brother and another part from another. Because of his many illnesses and the cold in his members, he would sometimes use new cloth for patching. He held to this sort of poverty in his clothing, and observed it until the year he passed to the Lord.

A short time before his death when he was badly dessicated from dropsy, and suffering many other illnesses, the brothers made several tunics for him so that they could make the changes night or day when needed.

Another time, a poor man, wretchedly clothed, came to a certain hermitage of the brothers to beg a bit of cloth from them for the love of God. St. Francis told one of the brothers to look around the house and see if he could find a length or a piece of cloth to give him. The brother searched the house but came back saying he had found nothing. So that the poor man would not have to go away empty-handed, St. Francis went secretly, so that his Guardian would not forbid what he was about to do, took a knife, sat down where he would not be seen, and began to detach a piece of cloth sewn to the inside of his tunic. He thought he could give it to the poor man in secret. However his Guardian was quick to realize what he was trying to do. He went to him and forbade him to give away that piece of cloth, for it was extremely cold at the time and St. Francis was suffering keenly from his illness in that cold. St. Francis told him, "If you want me not to give it to him, then absolutely you must have another piece given to Brother Pauper." Thereupon the brothers gave the poor man some cloth from their own clothing for St. Francis's sake.

After he had begun to be ill he was unable to travel on foot and sometimes had to go riding on a donkey. He would not go on horseback except in cases of the strictest and most extreme necessity. This he began to do only a short time before his death when his illness became very grievous. If he were going about to preach and was riding either an ass or a horse, or if he were staying at one of the brothers' places, and the brothers would lend him a cape, he would accept it only under a certain condition: if he were to come upon a very poor man, or if such a poor man were to come to him, he must be free to give the cape to that man if his spirit testified to him that it was clearly a case of necessity.

At one time, at the very beginning of the Order when St. Francis was staying at Rivotorto with two brothers, the only brothers he then had, a man came from the world wanting to adopt his way of life. He was the third brother.

He had been there for a few days, still wearing the clothes he had on when he came from the world, when a certain poor man came to that place begging alms of St. Fràncis. St. Francis told the one who was the third brother, "Give Brother Pauper your cloak." Immediately and cheerfully he took it from his back and gave it to the man. Since he had given his cloak to the man with joy, it seemed to him that the Lord had on that occasion straightway infused new grace into his heart.

On another occasion he was staying at the church of St. Mary of the Portiuncula when a certain aged and poverty stricken woman, who had two sons in the Order, came to the place to ask alms of St. Francis. She was in needy straits because that year she was without means of livelihood.

St. Francis said to Brother Peter Cattanii who was then Minister General, " Haven't we anything we can give our mother ? " St. Francis would call the mother of any of the brothers *Mother* as if she were his own mother and as if she were mother of all the brothers of the Order. Brother Peter answered, " There is nothing in the house to give her, especially as the alms would have to be considerable if she were to have enough to live on. In the church we have only one New Testament for reading the lessons at Matins. "

At that time the brothers had no breviaries and very few Psalters. Notwithstanding, St. Francis replied, " Give Mother our New Testament. She can sell it and get enough to take care of her needs. I firmly believe that this would please the Lord and his holy Virgin Mother more than your reading from it. " So he gave it to her.

It can truly be said and written of St. Francis what is said and read about Job: " Mercy came forth from the womb of my mother and grew along with me (*Job* 31,18)." For us who were with him, it would take a long time to write and narrate not only what we have heard from others about his charity and piety toward the poor, but as well all we have seen with our own eyes.

Two miraculous cures and a prophecy

Oxen are cured when sprinkled with water in which St. Francis had washed — a licentious priest is cured of a grave malady — on returning to sinful practices he is chastised as the Saint had foretold.

At that time, while St. Francis was staying at the hermitage of St. Francis of Fonte Colombo, the oxen of the nearby village of St. Elia were struck by a disease. It was commonly called *basabove*, a disease none of them could escape, and they all began to get sick and die.

One night it was told in a vision to a certain spiritual man of the village, "Go to the hermitage where St. Francis is staying. Get some water he has used for washing his hands and feet, and then throw it over the oxen. They will be healed immediately." The man arose early in the morning, went to the hermitage, and told St. Francis's companions all about it.

At mealtime they poured the water he had used for washing his hands into a jar. That evening they asked him to let them wash his feet, but making no mention of this affair. Afterwards they were able to give the man water in which St. Francis's hands and feet had been washed.

The man carried it away and sprinkled it, in the way one sprinkles holy water, over the oxen that lay almost dead, and over all the others too. Immediately, through the grace of the Lord and the merits of St. Francis, all were cured. At that time St. Francis had wounds in his hands, feet, and side.

During that time St. Francis's eyes were afflicted with his eye disease and he was staying a while in the bishop's palace at Rieti. A priest of the Rieti diocese named Gedeon, a very worldly-minded man, lay ill with a serious disease, suffering intense pain in the loins. He could neither move nor turn over in his bed without help, nor could he get up and walk, but had to have several people carry him. When he was carried he went bent over and doubled up because of the pain in his loins. He could not straighten himself up at all.

One day he had himself carried to St. Francis. He cast himself down at the holy Father's feet and tearfully begged him to make a sign of the cross over him. St. Francis told him, "How am I to make a sign of the cross over you ? Before you got your disease you always lived according to your fleshly desires with no thought nor fear of God's judgment." But seeing how badly he was afflicted by illness and pains, he was moved by pity for him and told him, "I will make a sign of the cross over you in the name of the Lord, but if it be the Lord's pleasure to heal you, take care not to return to your vomit. If you do return to your vomit, I tell you truly that something worse than you had before will come upon you, and you will incur an extremely harsh judgment for your sins, your ungratefulness, and your heedlessness of the Lord's great goodness."

As soon as St. Francis had made a sign of the cross over the man, he stood up straight, his internal ailments completely healed. As he straightened up, the bones of his loins made a sound like someone breaking dry sticks with his hands.

However, a few years later the man returned to his vomit and no longer minded what the Lord had told him through his servant Francis. One day he dined in the home of a fellow canon and slept in his house that night. It happened that the roof of the house suddenly collapsed. All the others escaped death; only this wretched man was trapped inside and killed.

The Lord answers a question for St. Francis

St. Francis has nothing to offer the Lord in exchange for a grace because he has already given him all — the Lord sets St. Francis's mind at rest with a simple reply.

One time St. Francis called his companions to him in the cell where he was staying and said, " Listen and give careful attention. I have asked the Lord in his mercy that he deign to make it clear to me when I am his servant and when I'm not, for I want always to be found his servant.

" It was told me in spirit, 'What will you give me if I make clear to you what you ask ?' And I said, 'Lord, I have given you my body and my soul; after this I have nothing left to offer you.' The Lord said, 'Such being the case, learn and know that you are truly my servant when you think what is good, speak what is good, and do what is good.'"

192

TOPICAL INDEX
A guide to key themes of the narrative

APOSTOLATE TO FOREIGN LANDS:

A decision is made in Chapter to send brothers to foreign lands, 113.

St. Francis affirms a universal mission for his Order, 118.

St. Francis feels obliged to go to a distant country so as to be an example for brothers in tribulation, 113, 118.

After prayer he decides to go on a mission to France because of Eucharistic devotion in that very Catholic country, 114.

The pope's representative forbids his leaving the country, 118-119.

Brother Pacificus heads the mission to France, 119.

St. Francis journeys to Egypt, 159.

BARGAINING:

A treasure is offered in exchange for tribulations, 168.

The treasure offered in recompense (cf. Kingdom of Heaven, a treasure, *Mt* 13,44,19,21, *Mk* 10,21, *Lk* 18,22) is supremely desirable and worth infinitely more than any possible earthly treasure, 168.

Sackcloth is profitable merchandise, 37.

Through death St. Francis will pass from extreme poverty to infinite riches, 43.

Alms given " for the love of God " acquires for the giver many times the value of what he gives, 7, 76-77.

Chastity is rewarded with a great recompense, 143.

The Lord will recompense brothers laboring for Francis during a troublesome illness, 178.

St. Francis has nothing left to offer in exchange for a grace, 192.

The performance of the Lord's ministrels is to be paid with penitential lives, 171.

The obedient subject will gain a reward, 31.

BEGGING:

Begging is a noble practice imitating the all-highest King who made himself poor and despised, 10.

Begging is a heritage and vocation of royal dignity proper to the brothers' vow, 7, 8, 10.

After original sin all men's possessions are received in alms from God through his Son's merit, 7.

Brothers should beg alms " for the love of God ", 11, 76.

The begging brother offers the alms-giver immense profit in acquisition of " the love of God ", 7, 76-7.

What is done for the Least Brothers (Friars Minor) is done for Christ, 18.

St. Francis begs bread when guest in homes of the wealthy to assure good example for the brothers, 7-8, 10-11.

Men of high station revere St. Francis's begged bread, 8, 9.

The brothers should beg and do so joyfully, 11-12, 77.

Ministers and preachers should beg, 25.

Only sufficient needs for the day should be begged, 77.

Soldiers accompanying St. Francis learn the excellence of begging " for the love of God ", 6.

Body:

St. Francis regarded his body as an enemy, 107-108.

The flesh is an opponent to God's gifts, 50.

The flesh is a seat of vanity, 121.

St. Francis and his companions treated the body harshly, even contrary to needs, 71, 72, 78.

The Passion of Christ is source of consolation in illness for St. Francis, 160.

St. Francis permitted the cure of his eyes under obedience, 166, 167, 177-178.

Counsels on mortification, 71-72, 74, 75, 86.

Bro. Bernard gives up rights over his body, 55-56.

Evidence of St. Francis's attention to bodily cleanliness, 190.

St. Francis was frail and ailing as a youth, and increasingly so as a Religious, 64-65, 75, 76, 188.

Buildings:

Agreement at Rivotortò on the necessity of a church and individual cells, 81-2.

The reasons for St. Francis's pleasure in St. Mary of the Angels, 83.

The proper materials for the brothers' houses, 82, 92-3, 95.

St. Francis's mind on buildings, 82, 89, 91-2, 93 ff.

Buildings not to be held with right of ownership, 94.

Churches should be small but kept clean, 95, 99.

CANTICLE OF BROTHER SUN:

(The Companions' text gives only the opening lines of the *Canticle* - the remainder is here translated from *Assisi Codex 338*).

St. Francis in torment is promised the recompense of a treasure which is the Kingdom of God, 168.

In joyous gratitude for the assured treasure he is inspired to compose the *Canticle*, 168-9.

He intends that the *Canticle* be sung, 170, 171.

Motives for composing the *Canticle*: The Lord's praise, his own consolation, and the people's sanctification, 169.

The singing of the Canticle turns his thoughts from his sufferings to joyous praise of the Lord, 13, 14, 172.

He teaches that gratitude to the Lord for good, useful and beautiful creatures demands praise of the Creator and Donor, 169, 172, 183.

Use of creatures contrary to the Creator's will offends him and is sin, 169.

The *Canticle* is basically a call to penitence - the brothers should first preach, and then sing the *Canticle;* they are like the Lord's minstrels (*ioculatores:* clowning acrobats, popular singers) stirring men to joyfulness, but joy in living according to the Creator's will, 171-2.

Especially Brother Sun and Brother Fire invite men to praise the Lord (as at Lauds and Vespers), 172.

He gives his composition a name, 172.

Stanzas composed for pardon and the welcome of Sister Death (verses from the Companions' text), 44, 173 ff.

CHURCH AND CHURCHMEN IN THE MIND OF ST. FRANCIS:

The brothers should be faithful and subject to bishops and priests of Holy Mother Church, 94-5.

St. Francis is respectful and obedient to the pope's representative, 9-10, 118-9, 166, 177.

He defends the brothers' vocation with deference before the pope's representative, 9-10, 118-9.

He is grateful for a bishop's disparagement, 49.

He is grateful for the counsel of the Bishop of Assisi, 95.

He acknowledges the authority of a bishop, 94-5.

He instructs the brothers to practice humble respect and service to prelates and priests, 95.

He teaches reverence of theologians but discourages his brothers' studies, 24.

He reproves a sinful priest, 191.

He admonishes priests but out of the faithful's hearing, 99.

CHURCHMEN WITH REGARD TO ST. FRANCIS:

The Bishop of Assisi was helpful - was the friend of St. Francis, he declares his holiness, 79, 95.

The Bishop of Ostia (later to become pope) is accustomed to receive him as a guest giving him a place of honor, 9, 10.

The Bishop of Ostia and his retinue are edified by the poverty of the brothers' furnishings, 151-2.

The representative of the pope exercises authority over him with friendliness and deference, 9, 10, 118.

The pope and other Roman prelates hold him in high esteem as a saint, 61-2.

He was considered a distinguished dignitary in the Church, 49.

The Bishop of Terni indicates him as a saint with a mission of renewing the faith of the Church, 49.

He is accorded prestige at the Roman Curia - he and his Order are opposed by some prelates at Rome, 118.

A priest accepts his counsel, 139.

An abbot loves and reveres him, 157.

CLARE: ST. CLARE, LADY CLARE, POOR CLARES:

The term " little plant " was St. Francis's term for St. Clare as well as the family of Poor Clares, 57, 88, 176.

St. Clare, like St. Francis, follows the exemplary " poverty of the Son of God ", 57.

Model brothers at St. Mary of the Angels will edify and protect the " little plant ", 88.

St. Clare has a brother take a message to " her one father after God, " expressing fear that she will not live to see him again, and he has a letter of consolation sent back to her, 57-8.

There were no visits between St. Clare or the poor Clares with St. Francis during his illness — they were hence not responsible for the invalid being housed in a place infested by mice — although the sisters practiced sewing daily the

198

brothers made a hood for St. Francis, thus marking independence from the sisters' care at St. Damien's, 176, 177.

The essential message sent to the Poor Clares - with a song, 175-6.

The place of the brothers' preaching and the Poor Clares' receiving Holy Communion is specified, and is reported as being thus used at the time of writing, 59.

COMMUNICATIONS FROM GOD:

St. Francis regularly sought and received the Lord's instructions, 20, 33, 41-2, 66-7.

A conflict of authority between the express will of the Lord and decisions based on learning, 33-34.

St. Francis willed that divine directions ignored by the brothers be fulfilled in his own assiduous practice of them, 20-1.

In a consoling message the Lord arrogates to himself the responsibility for the Order, 123-4.

The Lord's will discerned by opening a Gospel book, 27.

The Lord puts a problem of conscience at rest, 192.

St. Francis invokes the expression of the Lord's will, 41, 42.

Assurance of the Blessed Virgin's preference for her church of the Portiuncula, 85.

The Lord revealed the brothers' salutation: " May the Lord give you peace, " 18-19.

A message on faith brings peace to St. Francis, 104.

Mention of the encounter with the Seraph, 67.

The Kingdom of God is assured to St. Francis, 168.

The Lord indicates St. Francis's person to Pacificus, 109.

Pacificus receives a prophetic vision, 108.

A divine communication to Lady Jacoba, 46.

CREATURES IN THE MIND OF ST. FRANCIS:

He held creatures in great affection and reverence, and called them brothers and sisters because they are works of his Lord and Creator, 59-61, 121, 179, 180-1.

He had affection and reverence for creatures because of Scriptural reference to Christ (Ox and ass - Rock), 60, 182.

His spirit was lifted to contemplation of God through delight in creatures as exemplified in the *Canticle*, 172, 180-1.

He delighted in the goodness, charm and beauty of creatures in themselves, not only because of their relation to the Creator and the Christ, 67, 121, 180-1.

Creatures were created for man's service and hence are motive for men's praise and thanksgiving to their Creator, 169, 183.

The sun ranks highest among creatures: as a symbol it illustrates God's attributes, and it is the chief source of light, 172.

Particular appreciation of Brother Fire, 172, 179, 180-2.

Brother Fire kindly spares him pain, 179.

Homage of the larks for whom he had had affectionate regard, 59-61.

Different kinds of birds give him a sign and delight him, 67.

Sister Locust obediently responds to his request, 120-1.

Tormenting mice are a demoniacal temptation, 167.

He pities a lamb which symbolizes innocence and goodness and curses a sow symbolizing evil, 133.

He grieves on witnessing creatures mistreated, 180.

DEATH OF ST. FRANCIS:

For a number of years he had meditated upon his death, 14.

Awaiting death St. Francis was joyful because of union with God already achieved, 14.

He joyfully welcomes Sister Death and praises her with a new stanza for his *Canticle*, 16, 43-44.

The date of his death is foretold, 16.

He gives a final blessing to Assisi, 40.

Expecting death he provides a brother with a keepsake and acknowledges to another that his remains will be venerated as a relic, 37-38.

He willed to lay in death naked on the naked ground, 42.

Through the inspired devotion of Lady Jacoba he was worthily prepared for his funeral, 46-7.

A triumphal procession and a prophesied visit to St. Clare at St. Damien's, 59.

The rule and his teachings remain valid after his death, 126.

DEMONS AND TEMPTATIONS:

St. Francis explains the function of demons as agents of the Lord, 63-4.

Demons will punish unfaithful brothers, 32.

The devil combats saintly practices, 69-70, 71, 72.

Necessity of reacting quickly against the devil's suggestions, 71.

The demons torment physically, 63, 68.

A joyful heart is a defense against demons, 70-71, 72-3.

Mere suggestions of the devil need not be confessed by a tormented brother, 80.

Excessive labors become a temptation against spiritual fervor, 178.

Cruel demoniacal temptations at La Verna at the time of the Seraph's visitation, 67-8.

Bro. Leo's blessing written as remedy against temptation, 39.

St. Francis withdrew from the brothers' company when temptation rendered him unable to appear cheerful, 68, 103.

Books had been a temptation for St. Francis, 27.

St. Francis frees a brother from demoniacal temptation, 80-1.

The diabolical temptations of Bernard, 54 ff.

Sylvester exorcises demons from Arezzo, 116-7.

DRAMATIC EXPRESSION:

St. Francis kneels humbly before a brother and asks him to return to the place where a mistaken decision was made and there eliminates it, 28.

He rubs his head with ashes, 27.

He enacts a lesson on poverty and humility on Christmas day, 149-150.

He appears before the people stripped of his tunic being led with a rope around his neck, 161-163.

He rids himself of the bedcover he had denied Bro. Fire, 182.

He invokes a response from brothers by sitting naked on the ground and signifies ideal poverty, 41-2.

By significant action he transfers ownership of a tunic to a brother, 38.

He expresses contrition by eating from the same bowl as a leper, 106.

He breaks bread with brothers in a manner signifying that he includes all present, absent, and to come, 34.

A brother is instructed to enact his request for pardon, 127-8.

Brother Bernard has a Last Supper of cherries, 56.

In homage to poverty St. Francis offers begged bread to the Cardinal's distinguished guests, 9.

EXAMPLE AND MODEL:

The Lord's example is model for the brothers in living the life of holy poverty, 76.

St. Francis teaches his brothers by his deeds, 8, 9-10, 64, 118, 122-3, 126, 149-50.

St. Francis proclaimed gospel precepts deleted from the rule by Ministers through his own example of loyally practicing them, 22.

Because of the brothers' failure in good example, St. Francis resigned office but continued to teach and guide by his own example, 31-32.

St. Francis suffered bitterly from the brothers' bad example in behavior or by defection - when thinking himself " in extremis " he left a warning, 98, 126.

Directions for life at St. Mary of the Angels - it bore the obligation of being model and example for all other houses, 88, 91.

St. Francis intended to destroy a house which would give bad example and remonstrates with a Minister General who was constructing a useful building, 89-91.

Correction should be made through example rather than through punishment, 31.

Brothers preaching in churches of others rather than building large ones of their own thus give good example, 95-6.

St. Francis decided to go on a foreign mission to support other brothers with his example, 113, 118.

St. Francis publicly avows hidden faults for good example, 162, 164-5.

His good example bears fruit in compunction, 49, 163.

He must be a good example when dying, 44.

Sister Lark furnishes good example for Religious, 60-1.

FRATERNAL LOVE:

St. Francis celebrates brotherly love in the breaking of bread, 34-5.

Brother Bernard celebrates a Pasch of cherries with his brothers, 56.

St. Francis blesses all brothers - present, absent and to come, 34, 97-8.

Brothers should love and respect one another, and be subject one to another, 10, 98.

All brothers are as if sons of the same mother, 101, 189.

St. Francis honors Bernard, his first companion, with his greatest love, 53-4.

St. Francis ceded on rulings willed by the Lord to avoid dissension - he resigned government of the Order because he refused to practice harsh disciplinary measures, 31, 33, 34.

St. Francis won over the adverse sentiments of his companions with gentle, cheerful persuasion, 185.

St. Francis was sensitively compassionate to his brothers, 38, 39, 73-4, 78, 80, 129-30, 146-8, 178, 185.

St. Francis rejoiced in having good companions and was happy because of their virtues, 12, 54, 77, 100.

When temptation did not allow a cheerful spirit St. Francis was more rarely in the brothers' company, 68, 103-4.

FRIARS MINOR (LITTLE, LESSER, LEAST BROTHERS):

Scriptural sources for the name *Fratres Minores*, 17-18.

A *little* flock wanting no possession except Christ, 17, 19.

The name was divinely revealed to St. Francis, 18.

The name *Fratres Minores* was written in the rule submitted to Innocent III and was approved, 18.

The Friars Minor, identified with no social class, should be humble before all other people, 95.

St. Francis clarifies a distinction between himself and a man poor of necessity, 126-7.

The spiritual profit of the people is the purpose of the brothers' apostolate, 94.

The brothers should aid and be subservient to bishops and priests, 95, 98.

Brothers were received at St. Mary of the Angels and with St. Francis's approval, 90, 144.

The brothers are like popular entertainers of the Lord arousing spiritual joy, 171-2.

The Friars Minor have a universal mission, 118.

The Lord who founded the Order will sustain it throughout its vicissitudes to the end of the world, 124.

The Holy Spirit will continue to guide and teach the Friars Minor, 10.

St. Francis blesses present and future members of the Order but curses those who give bad example, 97, 98.

ILLNESSES OF ST. FRANCIS:

He was ailing as a youth and as a Religious, 64-5, 76, 161.

Illnesses: dropsy, diseased liver, spleen, stomach and eyes, 70, 159, 166.

Pus flowed over his eyes, 180.

In later years he could bear no light on his eyes, 167, 177.

In the period before his death his habit was changed often because of dropsy, 187.

Although always ailing and frequently grievously ill he was severe with himself and observed the rule strictly so as to aid the Brothers with good example, 20-21, 31-2, 122-3, 125-6, 161.

He obtained consolation in suffering from music, praises sung to the Lord, and meditation upon the Lord's Passion, 137, 159, 160, 169, 172.

He gave illness as reason for resigning office -- but he had major reasons, 30-1, 50-1, 52, 119-120, 125-6.

Normally he traveled on foot, when ill on a donkey, when extremely ill on a horse, 188.

Description of a crisis in his illness, 97.

JOY AND CHEERFULNESS:

Joy is the fruit of a chastened body and a pure heart, 72.

St. Francis claims a right to be joyful because of union with his Lord, 14.

Even in bad health poverty was practiced joyfully, 78.

St. Francis commends his brothers because they beg joyfully, 12, 77.

St. Francis joyfully deprived himself of necessary articles to give them to others, 185 ff.

A brother's joy in giving his cape is a sign of grace, 188.

A companion's cheerfulness is an aid to brothers enduring spiritual trials, 72-3.

St. Francis willed to be content with all that happened, 51-3.

Loss of joy gives the devil an entrance to the soul, 71-3.

Prudent care of body is required to permit joy in hardship, 71.

St. Francis withdrew from the brothers' company in a period when he could not be cheerful, 67-8, 103-4.

St. Francis reproves a brother for his sorrowful demeanor, 72.

St. Francis rejoiced because of good companions, 75.

The brothers have the vocation of arousing spiritual joy, 171.

Christians should exult and make the poor as well as birds and beasts happy on the feast of the Nativity, 60.

LEPERS:

(Care of lepers is the only work specified by St. Francis as a responsibility of the brothers in this narrative).

St. Francis recommended extreme cases of leprosy to Brother James who cared for them devotedly without thought for revulsion or danger to his person, 105.

St. Francis directs that the brotherly care of lepers be limited by prudence, 105.

St. Francis gives lepers the name " Brother Christians, " 105.

Commonly the people abhored badly ulcerated lepers, 105.

St. Francis directed that brothers, including those of noble families, should serve lepers for the sake of humility, 48.

St. Francis does a horrifying penance for offending the sentiments of a leper, 105-6.

Music:

St. Mary of the Angels should be sanctified with hymns and praises of the Lord, 87, 88.

Musical instruments are properly used for God's praise, 136-7.

Since most people do not understand divine things they make vain and sinful use of musical instruments, 137.

St. Francis immediately composed music for the *Canticle* and taught brothers to sing it, 170-1.

He composed a song for the consolation of the Poor Clares, 175.

He states motives for composition of his *Canticle:* the Lord's praise, his own consolation, and the people's sanctification, 169, 171.

He obtains consolation in pain from holy music, 13, 137, 170, 172.

The brothers are like the Lord's minstrels, 171.

An angel consoles him with zither playing, 137.

Brother Pacificus had been a celebrated singer, 107, 109.

A brother fears he will cause scandal if he borrows a musical instrument to accompany the *Canticle*, 136-7.

NOBLES AND WEALTHY MEN IN THE MIND OF ST. FRANCIS:

He accepts hospitality from noble, distinguished, and wealthy personages but insists upon begging to maintain a good example for the brothers, 7-8, 10.

He prefers the poor fare of the brothers to the fine foods at the tables of the rich, 10-11.

He places value on the regard of people in high station, 19, 76.

He relieves his wealthy doctor of the burden of a poor woman's daily expenses, 184.

He is considerate of a humiliated brother who had been of prominent family, 146-7.

NOBLES AND WEALTHY MEN WITH REGARD TO ST. FRANCIS:

Nobles and wealthy men are pleased to have him as guest, 9, 10.

Nobles and wealthy men are edified by his begging, 8, 10.

A nobleman concedes property to the brothers, 93.

A wealthy doctor marvels at his sanctity, 141, 179-80.

A wealthy doctor accepts the brothers' hospitality, 141.

OBEDIENCE AND AUTHORITY:

The subject should obey his Superior for love of the obedient Christ, 51-2.

St. Francis understood the office of Superior as a spiritual function, hence not to be exercised with recourse to harsh coercion proper to temporal governors, 31, 52.

St. Francis sounds a warning against the misuse of authority by superiors, 51.

A good subject readily obeys his Superior, 31.

St. Francis permitted medical attention to his person as an act of obedience, 166-7, 177.

For motives of succoring the needy poor or of penance St. Francis imposed his will on his Superior, 106, 162, 184-5-7-8-9.

St. Francis abandons a mission to France in obedience to the pope's representative, 118-9.

Through the virtue of obedience a brother miraculously finds parsley, but is reprimanded for not acting more readily, 35-6.

A worthy dinner is supplied for the doctor when the companions obediently make preparations, 140-1.

POOR - ST. FRANCIS'S RESPONSE TO POOR INDIVIDUALS:·

A wretched poor man mirrors the Incarnate Son of God, 127-8.

He is ashamed when he comes upon a man poorer than himself, 126-7.

He overcomes any impediments in giving alms to a needy individual, 183-5-6-7-8-9.

He is compassionate to the poor family of Simple John while defending John's will to become a servant of God, 100-1.

Beggars should sit with the brothers at table, 151.

He contrives a manner of being considerate to a poor woman's sensibilities in giving her alms, 183-4.

POVERTY AND HUMILITY (see also BEGGING and BUILDINGS):

Possession of the sovereignly desirable Person of the Son of God is the basic motive and specific aim of poverty in the mind of St. Francis, 17-8, 9.

The poor brothers have assurance of the Gospel that they will receive the Kingdom of Heaven - it is likened to an inestimable treasure on the occasion of composing the *Canticle*, 18, 168-9.

The brothers should follow the example of poverty and humility left them by the Son of God and his Blessed Mother, 48, 76, 150.

The exemplar is " the all-highest King, the Lord of all things... rich and glorious in majesty come among us... poor and despised ", 10.

Brothers must follow the Gospel selling all possessions and giving the proceeds to the poor for acceptance in the Order, 100, 102-3.

St. Francis founded the Order on the firm rock of poverty and humility exemplified by the Son of God, 48.

The poverty of the first brothers stands as model for succeeding friars, 23, 29, 30-31, 32, 89.

Small, poor houses are signs of poverty and humility, 32.

Large communities are not favorable for the practice of poverty, 94.

Books should not be possessed for reason of poverty and humility, 16-7, 21, 23, 26-7.

Compassionate love should be shown a poor, ailing man because he reflects the image of the Incarnate Son of God, 127-8.

St. Francis despoils himself of the privilege of choosing his companions, 52.

St. Francis wished to be treated as a pauper, 62.

St. Francis achieves his ideal of poverty when lying naked in death, 41-2.

Illustrations of St. Francis's practice of poverty in clothing, dwelling place, traveling, eating on the ground, etc., 64-5, 90-2, 151-2, 185-9.

PRAYER:

Characteristics of St. Francis's prayer

Joyful praise, 14, 168, 171-2, 181, 183.

United with the Lord, 14.

Indications of ecstatic prayer (as seen by the Bishop of Assisi, as presumed in the apparition of the Seraph, as supposed when aroused by the wonders of creatures), 67, 79, 181.

Torment by demons at periods of prayer, 65, 67, 68, 70.

Meditation on the Passion and other mysteries of the Incarnate Christ, 159-161.

Consolation obtained through prayer, 13-14, 107-8, 159-161, 172.

Divine communications received in prayer, 20, 66-7, 85, 123-4.

Temptation removed through prayer, 103-4.

Prayer to be made aware of his sin, 64.

Prayer to be freed of wrath or rancor, 52.

He implores divine aid for the Order, 33, 125.

He implores guidance for government of brothers, where to go, what to do, etc., 20, 33, 66-7, 113-4.

Consolation given when suffering for defecting brothers, 123-4.

Prayer for benefit of souls, 156, 157-8.

Prayer offered as soon as possible after a request for it is made by someone for the good of his soul, 158.

The Nativity was his preferred liturgical feast, 60.

Devotion to the Eucharist, 99, 114-5.

His prayer for the Lord's blessing of Assisi, 40-1.

In solitude

He liked La Verna because it was secluded, 66.

He preferred secluded places and solitude for prayer, 62, 63, 65, 107, 147-8, 152.

His cell was separate from the brothers' houses at St. Mary of the Angels, Greccio, La Verna, 68, 79, 120, 182.

Manner of praying

A reason for acquiring St. Mary of the Angels was the need for a place to recite the Divine Office, 82.

Provisions for the exemplary chanting of the Divine office at St. Mary of the Angels, 87.

Set times for prayer and office, 70, 115, 153, 167.

Mention of Tierce, Compline and Matins, 69, 77, 107, 115.

Disciplined posture in prayer, 70.

Inner quiet for prayer, 70, 95, 115.

He wanted to assist at Mass or have the day's Gospel read, 97, 181.

In prayer before the altar, 108.

Various persons in prayer

The long prayer vigils with tears of a tempted Brother, 129.

An ecstasy and prophetic vision of Pacificus in prayer, 108.

Conversions are obtained by prayers of the " Knights of the Round Table " in solitude, 24-5.

Brother Bernard wishes nothing to disturb his meditations upon God, 55.

Prayers said by the Brothers as penances, 111-2.

Lady Jacoba prays with tears, 45.

The people of Greccio pray with the Brothers, 153.

An abbot experiences rapture, 158.

PREACHING:

St. Francis traveled about preaching, 7, 127, 130, 186.

Learned preachers are in danger of losing vocation, 24.

Preachers must not neglect prayer, should beg and do manual work, 25.

The vanity of preachers who take credit for recounting glorious deeds done by others, 26.

A preacher's merits are measured by his deeds, 28-9.

Fruits of preaching are earned by unknown " Knights of the Round Table ", 24-5.

Preaching to large assemblies to be done in the churches of others for humility's sake, 95-6.

In imitation of the Lord, St. Francis is called to both preaching and prayer in solitude, 66-7.

St. Francis preached penitence and contempt of world, 110, 154, 156.

214

St. Francis preached peace, 116-7, 155-6.

To priests he preached salvation of souls, 99.

The preaching of St. Francis and the brothers at Greccio, 153.

St. Francis sought the Lord's will on where he should go to preach, 113.

RULE:

Instructions obtained by St. Francis from the Lord through arduous prayer, 20, 32, 33-34.

St. Francis intended literal observance of the rule regarding poverty, 17, 20-1, 28.

The Religious are properly governed by observing the rule to which they are vowed, 21, 126.

Instructions imparted by the Lord were ignored or omitted from the rule with St. Francis's acquiescence to avoid dissension, 20, 22, 33-4.

Reverent care of the Blessed Sacrament prescribed by the rule, 114.

St. Francis willed that at death he would be poorer than poverty required by the rule, 42.

SACRED SCRIPTURE:

St. Francis was faithful to the literal sense of Scripture texts, 15, 77, 92, 182.

The rule requires following the Gospel scrupulously, 21, 22.

An exception made to a literal application, 101.

St. Francis had the Gospel of the day read when he could not assist at Mass, 181.

Meditation on the Lord is preferred to Scripture reading, 160-1.

Giving in alms of a New Testament book is better than reading it, 188-9.

Study of Scripture is threat to religious virtue, 24.

Genesis 1,27-30 and *Wisdom* 9,2 are reflected in St. Francis's understanding of creatures, 169, 183.

The *Thau* (see *Ezekiel* 9,4,6) distinguishes St. Francis, 110-1.

SERVANT OF GOD:

The servant of God is honored because of God's work through him, 50.

The servant of God is quick to destroy the devil's work, 70-1.

Servants of God should be peacemakers, 173.

Servants of God are joyful both in tribulation and in well-being, 72.

Servants of God, like minstrels (*joculatores*: clowning acrobats, popular singers) of the Lord, call men to joy in the Lord, through penitence, i.e. living according to God's will, 171.

How the servant of God deals with his body, 71-72.

When St. Francis is God's servant, 192.

A married lady wants to serve God, 142-3.

How girls served God living at home in Greccio, 153.

To serve God is to reign, 101.

SINFUL PEOPLE:

St. Francis tells his brothers how to win bandits to the Lord's service through brotherly charity, 130 ff.

St. Francis is merciful to an ailing priest but calls him to repentance for sin, 191-2.

St. Francis has the people of Arezzo and Greccio delivered from catastrophe but preaches repentance to them, 117, 153-4.

Through his words and virtues St. Francis reconciles a sinful man to God and his wife, 142-4.

SOCIETY IN GENERAL:

St. Francis had left the world and family along with relative fortune and state in life, 68-9, 75, 76, 95.

Lesser Brothers should be humble before all people, 95.

All men without regard for their station in life were called by St. Francis and his brothers to penitence and humble service of God, 7-8, 8-9, 94-5, 99-100.

He preaches against strife and immorality in society, 117, 153-5, 155-6, 171.

He instructs the brothers to preach to all through the example of their poor way of life, 95-6, 151-2.

He resisted popular admiration, 48-50, 161-4.

Pastoral sentiments even in tribulation, 6, 169, 171-2, 173-4.

SPIRIT: HOLY SPIRIT - TRANSPORT OF THE SPIRIT:

Transport of the spirit, 6, 14, 27, 38, 44, 118.

Knowledge through action of the Holy Spirit, 12, 22, 24, 54, 55, 129, 130.

The Holy Spirit teaches, 10, 14.

The Holy Spirit inspires alms-givers in response to requests " for the love of God ", 6.

The Holy Spirit had suggested meditation upon death to St. Francis, 14.

Assurance of the Kingdom given through God's Spirit, 168-9.

The Holy Spirit united St. Francis with the Lord, 14.

Announcement of the Order's universality made in a transport of the spirit, 118.

A prophecy to St. Clare by virtue of the Holy Spirit, 58.

A fleshly-minded candidate lies to the Holy Spirit, 144-5.

STIGMATA:

Description of circumstances at La Verna at the time of receiving the stigmata, 66-8.

The Companions testify to the stigmata, and to a miracle worked through water in which the Saint's wounded hands and feet have been washed, 190, 191.

TALKING:

St. Francis sought the quiet of solitude, 62-3, 65.

The soul in the body is like a hermit in a cell, 115.

Silence is to be fostered - useless talk to be avoided, 86.

Regulations governing speech, 111-2.

Talk about worldly affairs is forbidden, 87.

Norms for talking when journeying, 115.

Vow:

Brothers have the guidance of the rule because they are bound to its observance by vow, 125-6.

The Brothers of the earliest days are a model because of meticulous observance of their vow, 29-30.

St. Francis could have continued to govern the Order if the brothers had been true to their vow, 30.

The Lord Himself calls the brothers to the Order, gives the strength to persevere, and chastises defections, 123-4.

Disloyalty to the vow by transgressing God's commandments will be punished through the agency of demons, 32.

Example of a brother's wretched fate who defected from his vow, 135-6.

The vow obliges observance of poverty as literally stated in the Gospel, 21, 28.

St. Francis insists upon loyalty to the poverty vowed by the brothers, 8.

Because of having vowed poverty St. Francis is ashamed before a man poorer than himself of necessity, 126-7.

St. Francis enacts an example of a brother practicing the poverty to which he is vowed, 150.

Property used should be in keeping with the poverty vowed, 94, 96.

Work:

Servile work gives good example, 12.

St. Francis did manual work to counteract laziness, 111.

Ministers and preachers should do servile work for good example and for spiritual profit, 25.

The brothers did manual work to mortify the flesh and avoid idleness, 86.

Food given not as payment but as alms " for the love of God " to brothers laboring in the fields, 86.

St. Francis swept churches, 99.

Brothers, including those of noble family, should serve lepers for the sake of humility, 48.

INDEX OF PERSONS AND PLACES

Abbot, an, 157, 158.

Abbot of Subasio, 82, 83, 84.

Angelus, Bro, 3, 44, 62, 63.

Arezzo, 15, 116.

Assisi, 5, 13, 40, 57, 83, 88, 89, 90, 99, 146, 147, 162, 165, 173.

Bagdad, 37.

Bagnara, 13.

Benedict of Piracro, Bro., 97.

Bernard, Bro., 3, 53, 54, 55, 56.

Bishop of Assisi, 79, 82, 95, 173, 174.

Bishop of Ostia, 8, 9, 11, 117, 118, 151, 166, 177.

Bishop of Terni, 49.

Bishop's palace, Assisi, 13, 29, 37, 145, 174.

the same place, 38, 40, 145.

Bonaventure, Lord, 93, 97.

Borgo San Sepolcro, 130.

Bovara, 107.

Canons of St. Rufinus, 81, 82.

Caserta, 128.

Celle of Cortona, 142.

Charles, Emperor, 26.

Clare, Lady, Saint, 57, 58, 59.

Contigliano, 122.

Crescentius, Bro., 3.

Egypt, 159.

Elias, Bro., 13, 177.

Finiatu, 15.

Florence, 117, 118.

Foligno, 14.

Fonte Colombo, 65, 140, 190.
France, 114, 118, 119.
French Brothers, 186.

Gedeon, priest, 191.
Gerard, Bro., 146.
Giles, Bro., 3, 54.
Greccio, 4, 68, 147, 152, 153.
Gregory, Pope, 151.
Gubbio, 133.

Honorius, Pope, 117, 138.
Hugolin, Bishop, 61, 117.

Illuminatus of Arce, Bro., 3.
Innocent III, Pope, 18.

Jacoba, Lady, 45, 46, 47.
James, Bro., 105, 106.
John of Greccio, Lord, 68.
John, Bro., 3.
John, Simple, 99, 100, 101, 102.

Knights of the Round Table, 25.

Leo, Bro., 3, 44.
Leo, Cardinal, 61, 62, 63, 64, 65.

Lesser Brothers, Friars Minor, 17, 18, 21, 28, 48, 56, 84, 95, 119, 120, 171.
Lisciano, 142.
Lombardy, 117.
Lucca, 144.
Lucifer, 108, 109.

Machilone, 183.
March of Ancona, 16, 107, 109.
March country, 107.
March of Treviso, 118.
Masseus of Marignano, Bro., 3.
Mayor of Assisi, 90, 173, 174.
Minister General, 3, 23, 51, 52, 54, 85, 87, 88, 135, 162, 167, 177, 185, 189.
Mount Alverna, 39, 66, 181.

Nocera, 5.

Oliver, 26.

Pacificus, Bro., 107, 108, 109, 110, 119, 171.
Peregrinus of the Marches, Bro., 56.

Perugia, 155.
Peter Catanii, Bro., 50, 106, 162, 189.
Phillip, Bro., 3.
Poor Ladies, 175.
Poverty, Lady, 8, 24, 98.
Preggio, 142.

Rainerius, Bro., 120.
Richer, Bro., 16, 20.
Rieti, 65, 122, 136, 140, 147, 183, 191.
Rivotorto, 12, 73, 188.
Rocca di Bricio, 127.
Roland, 26.
Rome, 45, 61, 70, 118.
Rufinus, Bro., 3.

St. Damien, church, 57, 59, 167, 176.
   the same place, 175, 177.
St. Eleutherius, 122.
St. Elia, 190.
St. Fabian, church, 138.
St. Mary of the Angels (Portiuncula), 5, 12, 25, 28, 32, 40, 41, 50, 83, 84, 85, 88, 91, 99, 103, 104, 105, 111, 119, 151, 160, 188.
   the same place, 113, 120.
St. Rufinus, church, 81, 82, 162.
St. Verecundius, 133.
Siena, 5, 93.
Spoleto, Duchy, 117.
Spoleto, Valley, 84, 107, 119.
Sultan, 159.
Sylvester, Bro., 116, 117.

Tabaldus the Saracen, 136.
Terra Laboris, 128.
Terni, 49.
Trevi, 107.
Treviso, 118.
Tuscany, 117.

Venetian border, 118.

Arti Grafiche Antica Porziuncola
Finito di stampare nel mese di novembre 2003
Cannara (Perugia)